REA

ACPL ITEM

DISCARDE

D0942284

LOVE at first sight

JUL 1 7 2004

LOVE at first sight

SUZI MALIN

LONDON, NEW YORK, MELBOURNE, MUNICH, and DELHI

*Dedicated with love to my mother
and to my husband and two children*

Project Editor Diana Rayner
Project Designer Jo Grey
Managing Editor Gillian Emerson Roberts
Managing Art Editor Karen Sawyer
Category Publisher Mary-Clare Jerram
US Editor Margaret Parrish
DTP Designer Sonia Charbonnier
Picture Researcher Melanie Watson
Production Controller Joanna Bull

First American Edition, 2004

Published in the United States by
DK Publishing, Inc.
375 Hudson Street
New York, New York 10014

04 05 06 07 08 09 10 9 8 7 6 5 4 3 2 1

Copyright © 2004 Dorling Kindersley Limited
Text copyright © 2004 Suzi Malin

All rights reserved under International and Pan-American
Copyright Conventions. No part of this publication may be
reproduced, stored in a retrieval system, or transmitted
in any form by any means, electronic, mechanical,
photocopying, recording, or otherwise without the
prior written permission of the copyright owners. Published in
Great Britain by Dorling Kindersley Limited.

A Cataloging-in-Publication record for this book is
available from the Library of Congress.

ISBN 0-7566-0401-X

Color reproduced by Colourscan, Singapore
Printed and bound by Graphicom, Italy

Discover more at
www.dk.com

Contents

PRIMA COPULISM 100

HAVING IT ALL 144

DO WE HAVE IT? 164

In my own words

One might suppose that a painted portrait and a photographic portrait are created with the same goal in mind: to convey a likeness of the sitter. But there is an essential and important difference between the two. The portrait painter can isolate an expression captured in the eyes at any given moment and marry it with a fleeting expression in the mouth seen at another time. Hence, the artist conveys what he or she perceives about the sitter's personality, be it wisdom, kindness, humility, or any one of a hundred attributes. In this way the painter is able to impart layers of information about a person within a single painting so that the viewer receives so much silent data that they "know" the sitter and are at once intimate with the essence of the subject. This is not distortion, but merely artistic interpretation.

The photographer traps the expression of the eyes and the mouth at exactly the same time, freezing reality in a single moment. Here lies the difference: a photograph captures reality, while a painting is the artist's interpretation of it. Working with other people's photographs is rather like working with *objets trouvés*—found objects. The French artist Marcel Duchamp (1887–1968) worked with found objects. He had nothing to do with their creation; his art lay in the reinterpretation of those objects. The photographs I have used in this book are also "found" and, therefore, not styled for my use or taken with lighting to suit my convenience. Executed by others, cut up and reformed to create a new singular entity, these photographs assume a life of their own.

MY BACKGROUND AS A PAINTER

I specialize in portraying men. For most of my adult life I have sat in a studio, observing and painting. I have attempted to understand the mystery of the face and to penetrate its unspoken depths. In the face, repeated rhythms emerge: physical echoes, genetic patterns, and mathematical forms. I always try to gain an insight into the sitter's inner mechanism, which helps me to depict his image. I arrange to meet his wife, and this frequently helps toward an insight into the inner man, the "adult child" within. My sitter furnishes me with photographs of his parents, in particular of his mother. This is important because I can see how much of his face is inherited and how much is shaped by the man himself, his environment, and his experiences.

Some years ago, I began to notice the facial patterns of my sitter and how they appeared to affect his choice of partner. I became aware of the shapes and proportions within his wife's face, his mother's, and his own. It was like pieces in a jigsaw and, in anticipation of meeting a wife, I had an idea of what she might look like. Character is usually written in the eyes, while nature is seen around the mouth. The face does not lie, and much is written there. George Orwell said that by the time we reach 40, our faces can be read like a book. As an artist, however, I will not have had the benefit of reading the preceding chapters of the book—the sitter's emotional and family history. It is the photographs of parents and weddings that are my reference.

THE JOURNEY BEGINS

While I was at the Slade School of Fine Art in London, I wrote to the painter Lucian Freud who then visited me in my studio. After reviewing my work, he advised me not to be influenced by the Euston Road School, which advocated a mathematical approach to painting, if I was not happy working in that way. He recommended that I paint one area of the face to completion before going on to the next. I began to work additively, feeling my way slowly around the sitter's face, understanding each little part before continuing further. Working in this way led me to become a painter of detailed realism. As I became more familiar with each sitter, gaining greater insight into his personality and character, I was fascinated by how these were expressed on the face. For me, every face is a landscape, and I explore every inch of it as my eyes pass over its hills and valleys. Every feature and the spaces in between are instilled with meaning, and pieced together they brought me a little closer to understanding what it is that makes each person fascinating and unique. Ultimately, this led me to the discovery of the three visual love categories: harmonism, echoism, and prima copulism.

MOMENT OF TRUTH

I could not hear him. I could not smell him. I could only see him. From 30 yards away, across the lobby of a crowded room, I fell in love. No moment affected my life more. We were married exactly four weeks to the day that we met. That was almost 20 years ago. Why him? Why me? What was it that drew me? Instant recognition? Magic? A unique bond? Perhaps love's magic is not a mystery after all, but initiated by visual forces. Perhaps whom we choose to love is not so random, but destined from the cradle.

Seeking love and its meaning

The word "love" means different things to different people. When a person tells someone, "I love you," what that person means by love, and what the recipient expects from love, may differ widely, running the full gamut from the unconditional love that a parent may have for a child to sentiment, habit, passion, physical longing, emotional dependence, and so on.

Although I have named my three visual groups the "love categories," of course they could just as easily be called "attraction categories." It is only human to hope that initial attraction may be the starting point to lasting love.

How many times have you looked at a couple and wondered, "what does she see in him, or he in her?" The visual love categories revealed in *Love at First Sight* seek to explain what one person "sees" in another. As you peruse the studies in the book, bear in mind that visual attraction is only the starting point for a love match. Personality, character, integrity, wit, charm, sense of humor, charisma, sexual attraction, and so many other attributes and behavioral characteristics are the necessary components of any successful and enduring partnership. To suppose (or hope) otherwise would be foolish.

This book is not suggesting for one moment that by having harmonism, echoism, or prima copulism with a person, a successful love match or relationship will automatically ensue. But by being alive to them and including them in our awareness, we can perhaps come a little closer to understanding the visual triggers of attraction that may lead to love.

My research has shown that the three visual love categories apply to all, be they young or old, thin or fat, pretty or plain, straight or gay. Everyone has their match. Just as there are rhythms in nature, so too are there rhythms in the face. Everyone's physiognomical match is out there, waiting to discover its complement.

I am an artist by instinct and profession, and neither psychologist nor anthropologist, yet studying the visual nature of attraction has led me to ponder how it might be associated with the behavioural aspects of love. Perhaps the visual manner in which a man is attracted to a woman determines the kind of love he comes to feel for her. In other words, is how a person is loved a consequence of how they were first attracted to their partner in the beginning? Might men and women assume different roles according to the visual category in which that love occured? Might a woman be a different person if she were loved in a harmonist way; how might she behave if she were loved in an echoist manner? Would a man have the same love relationship with his harmonist match as with his prima copulist match? I continue to ponder these questions.

A great many people find love and happiness for reasons that have nothing to do with the visual love categories. They may have a joint passion for ornithology, a mutual interest in music, or enjoy shared intellectual endeavour. This "rational" love is an evolving love, based on warmth and friendship. Its beginnings are slow and steady but it can be as strong as the love that has its beginnings in visual attraction (see p. 11 slow love).

THE CATEGORIES EMERGE

I was painting a portrait of Diana, Princess of Wales after her death. Every time I lowered my head from the canvas to my palette, I caught sight of a picture of Prince Charles that was staring at me from the front page of a discarded newspaper. I did this so frequently that after a while, their images seemed to merge.

The similarities I had noticed in Charles and Diana led me to reexamine other couples in the hope of finding a pattern. Over the years I have painted numerous portraits. Photographs of these and my own photographic library gave me the opportunity to cut up, compare, and analyze thousands of images of facial features, especially noses, eyes, and mouths.

Strong patterns began to fall into place and thus the first category emerged: harmonism, in which the key facial characteristics of two people have similar proportions but are not similarly shaped.

Some while later, a photograph in a weekend newsapaper captioned, "Who is this?" caught my eye. The picture was of a woman wheeling a pram. I could see at once that it was Camilla Parker Bowles as a young woman. I was wrong. The photograph was of Prince Charles's nanny, Mabel Anderson, shown there in her twenties, at approximately the same age as Camilla was when she first met Charles. Many people have asked how the most eligible man in the world, married to the most glamorous woman in the world, could love another. The answer perhaps lay in the cradle. I knew that Sigmund Freud had written about attachment to the first bond (prima copula). Complex and complicated, the relationship with this significant figure colors all subsequent relationships. I was instantly struck with the possibility that there could be a visual trigger in later years to this first emotional bond. After examining many more couples for this link, the second category emerged: prima copulism, in which a person is attracted to someone who resembles their first bond.

The third category was much more difficult to establish. Plato claimed that God punished our earliest ancestors by cutting each in half. They longed to be reunited with their "other half," and when they found it fell in love. I had already identified that certain couples looked alike, but it was difficult to trace any pattern or to determine which particular "visual echoes" were the dominant ones in showing similarity between two people.

After analyzing hundreds of "similar looking" couples, I was amazed to discover that it was always the same three shapes that contributed most to their likeness: features that appeared to "echo" from the face of one partner to that of the other. Thus emerged echoism, the third and most common of the visual love categories.

Visual attraction *is just the starting point for a love match. Integrity, humor,* ***and other attributes*** *are* ***necessary components*** *of any lasting partnership.*

The three visual love categories

HARMONISM proportion

In harmonism, the two people will share similar facial proportions. This means that the relative distances between the forehead and bridge of nose, base of nose and mouth, and mouth and chin will be approximately the same. This is a subconscious mathematical pairing of physical types. When the distances between the main facial features are similar, the underlying head shapes are the same. Note that harmonists do not resemble each other unless they also have a degree of echoism.

ECHOISM shape

In echoism, the two people will resemble each other. The resemblance is caused by the echo of the shapes seen in three particular features. They are the upper eyelid line (from which the upper eyelashes grow), the upper lipline (the curve of pink lip on the edge where it meets the "moustache area"), and the eyebrow (not its upper or lower line but its general shape or sweep). The relative size of the features is not relevant: it is the shapes alone that determine echoism. Bear in mind also that the thickness of the lips does not signify. Lips thin with age and it is worth remembering this if one of the two people is older. The best echoist match is made with all three markers present. Two may suffice, but the echoism may be less strong.

PRIMA COPULISM first bond

In prima copulism, a person will be attracted to someone who resembles their first bond. For men, the first bond is most likely to have been his mother or other close female relative, or perhaps his nanny; for women, it is usually her father or other close male relative. Facial proportions and shapes are not relevant: the resemblance lies in the "look" or demeanor of a person. In both harmonism and echoism, the attraction is often mutual because the one subconsciously recognizes similar proportions or shapes in the other's face. In prima copulist love, the object of desire usually does not feel reciprocal attraction at the start. A man cannot be won over, but a woman may eventually be.

HAVING IT ALL

Can we have it all? The answer is affirmative since a couple may have aspects of all three visual love categories. For example, if a man's female partner resembles his first bond (say, his mother) there is a prima copulist element in the relationship. If the couple also share a degree of harmonism and echoism, then they are fortunate to have it all. There are of course different permutations of prima copulist love. With modern perspectives on sexuality, other interpretations of the first bond may bring new dimensions to the concept of "having it all."

3 1833 04659 8972

My concept of the visual love categories emerged from *years of painting men* and noticing how their *facial patterns* appeared to affect their *love choices*.

HOW WE FALL IN LOVE

Much research has been conducted into what attracts men and women to each other and how we fall in love. It is generally agreed that a man falls in love first with what he sees but that a woman can be "won over" by a man to whom she is not initially attracted.

Even when physical attraction and appeal are important to a woman, they have (at least in the early stages of a relationship) a far greater significance for a man. Indeed, if a man finds a woman attractive, it may not mean that he wants to get to know her or is looking for a deeper relationship with her. For men, then, the initial visual stimuli are the springboard from which a relationship may develop, given time. For many women, the way a man treats her and the way in which he responds to her can create the right emotional "climate" from which a physical attraction to him evolves.

Social psychologist Ayala Malach Pines has conducted extensive research into the gender processes of falling in love. In *Falling in Love: Why We Choose the Lovers We Choose*, she explains it like this: "A significant difference divided the genders. Men were more often initially attracted to the physical appearance of the woman, followed by a discovery of their personalities. Women, on the other hand, frequently felt no attraction. The attraction followed the development of friendship and emotional intimacy. To put it bluntly, for men the physical attraction caused the relationship; for many women the relationship caused the physical attraction." Similarly, Bertrand Russell wrote (1930) in *Conquest of Happiness*: "on the whole women tend to love men for their character, while men tend to love women for their appearance."

The nonvisual category

SLOW LOVE

In addition to the visual love categories, there is one other love group which has to do with a "nonvisual" attraction between two people. This does not for one moment mean that the partners are not attractive, merely that the way they look is not fundamental to their coupling. I have called this slow love.

People in the slow love category do not have any facial similarities at all, either in the shapes of their main features or in the proportions on their faces. Nor does prima copulism play a part, since neither partner will resemble the other's first bond. Slow love is an attraction based on warmth and friendship. It is an evolving love, often unrecognized by the two people in its early stages. Then it may begin to dawn on the couple that the other person could indeed be "the one" for them.

This love category is often based on shared interests or lifestyles—a hobby, profession, politics, background, or religion—and is an altogether more "rational" love than that of the visual categories. Its foundations tend to be firm, grounded in reality, unlike the instant and urgent love of prima copulism.

Often two people who have the same goals and aspirations can be united within this category. Theirs is a partnership of shared horizons, and because of this the couple can devote themselves to the practicalities of life and overcome its everyday hurdles outside the intimacy of the home.

Some words in conclusion

HAPPY EVER AFTER

Love has become part of our popular culture. If it were an industry, it would probably be the most profitable one of all time. Love sells magazines, films, and books. Longing for it, celebrating it, mourning its loss have become the background music of our lives.

We hear so much about "love" that it is easy to get things out of perspective. But the success of a relationship depends not simply on being able to give and receive love. As a couple we need to stay constant and weather the storms that life throws at us. When things get rough, it is good to remember that love flourishes best in a climate of trust and mutual respect. No matter how strong the initial attraction and how deep a love develops, nobody can predict the future of a relationship. Some partners can handle major storms and emerge stronger as a couple; others founder on the rocks of a minor transgression. The burden of celebrity may not be an issue for you, but it can put a great strain on the relationship of those in the spotlight.

CHANGING YOUR LOOKS

Many people turn to cosmetic procedures or surgery to improve aspects of their looks with which they are unhappy, or to cheat nature and slow the aging process. But can this affect the responses of those we would wish to attract?

The journey of this book is the belief that the face carries the past history and present identity that subconsciously attract another who recognizes these markers. Cosmetic surgery may change the face in such a way that it no longer reflects the true inner person.

It is rare that surgically altering one feature does not affect surrounding areas of the face, and changes to these areas may remove even more details of personal description. Nose surgery can sometimes alter the inner corner of the eye and its surrounding areas. This will of course influence the overall appearance of the eye. Sometimes more than one procedure will be carried out at the same time which will impact on different areas of the face. This can radically affect a person's ability to determine the individual and unique identity of another through the subconscious reading of the face. In effect it will present partners or potential partners with a "false" reading of a person's inner mechanism.

The response to a surgically altered face and its changed characteristics varies within each of the visual love categories. Trying to match features that may never be the same again may lead to disappointments. In the harmonist group, however, a reading will not be affected unless the proportions of the underlying bone structure are altered. It is as well to remember that in echoist attraction, there is a distinct and positive advantage to having a face that does not conform to popular ideals of physical perfection. The less surgically altered the face, the easier it is for the subconscious to identify the echoes within the face.

Alteration to the peripheries of the face does not affect the look of its center. In other words, neck lifts, ear pinning, and lower chin work should not affect the initial response to the face. Neither does surface surgery such as the removal of moles or scars, or dermabrasion.

> *The journey of this book* is the belief that the face carries past history and **present identity**. What is it **within the face** that stirs another to love?

PEOPLE WATCHING PEOPLE

Across the world, the phenomenon of the "cafe society" or culture has grown in recent years. Many a happy hour can be filled with pleasure just watching people go by.

Now this idle pleasure can be transformed into an engaging pastime. The revelations brought about by identifying the visual love categories afford the added pleasure of trying to pair two people and determine into which visual love category a couple may fit. Of course you will not be able to determine a possible prima copulist attraction just from seeing a couple on their own, but if the two people are part of a family group, it can be fascinating to try to work out what relationship there is between them, and if any prima copulism exists.

Attempting to spot a harmonist match can be more difficult. It is not easy to try to gauge proportions while sitting in a bar or waiting for a train unless you have been trained in visual processes. While you are looking through the studies in this book, you will notice that I have frequently provided information about the visual similarities of a couple in addition to the shape and proportion markers that determine an echoist or harmonist match. This may help you to "get your eye in" as you are learning to recognize the basic criteria for finding a match. Once these are established, it becomes quite easy to notice other similarities in a couple.

Echoism is by far the largest category within the visual love groups, and echoist couples are undoubtedly the easiest to spot. Remember that at least two out of the three markers are necessary to establish a match, and that the relative size of the features is not important. A couple with large eyes and small eyes can still have echoism as long as the shape of the upper eyelid line is the same.

In researching *Love at First Sight*, I have come across countless examples of echoist pairings among well-known people and celebrities in popular magazines and the society pages of glossy periodicals. Many appear in this book, and with good reason, since their inclusion serves a valid purpose. High-profile celebrity couples are apparently a source of endless fascination. How they live, what they do, and why they stay together makes for absorbing (if at times incredulous) reading. Reading about the visual love categories, and how people fit into them, would not be nearly so interesting if one knew nothing about the couple's lives.

There is a tendency in life to see only what we wish to see. By the use of photography, you can study what may not be available to the naked eye, thereby focusing on faces frozen in the same perspective. An entire book may be required to explain, deny, or justify the pull of a relationship. A single photograph can offer a glimpse of reality that tells all.

Harm

onism

When a man or woman is attracted to their harmonist match, there is a good chance that the attraction will be reciprocated because both parties will share the same characteristics of facial proportion.

What is a harmonist?

A harmonist has a face that shares the same proportions as that of their partner. They do not have similarly shaped features, but the spacing and distance between their key features is similar. Partners with harmonism may not look alike, so a harmonist couple is not easy to spot at a glance.

What is harmonism?

Harmonism occurs when individuals unwittingly pair with someone who has similar facial proportions. They like the way the other person looks and feel physically compatible. Harmonists often complement each other socially, each drawing strength and confidence from the other's presence.

For people who are shy by nature, it is a tremendous bonus to have a partner with whom they feel comfortable when they appear in public. Many high-profile individuals who feel lonely or isolated by their celebrity status choose harmonist partners. As often as not, these celebrity couplings tend to be based on aesthetics and such couples fit well together within their social group.

Harmonism can and does work for many couples, but it also suffers a high casualty rate because the initial relationship is based on looks. Time erodes beauty, and unless the partners are fortunate enough to find the "beauty within," their love may ultimately dwindle or die. For the majority, however, harmonism works well, and not being in the limelight is a blessing if difficulties do occur.

Some harmonist women work hard to stay attractive (the cosmetics industry thrives on harmonist love) and the aging process may cause great anxiety within this group. Many "trophy wives" fall into this category; often they may become aware of an emotional loneliness or a feeling that something is missing. Sometimes their partners do not respond in the way they would wish. They are together but alone, and the harmonist relationship may sometimes be a cold coupling.

Harmonist couples may have a relationship that lasts beyond its natural life. In the case of celebrities, the media often extend the period of this relationship, since the pair are seen to be "the perfect couple," and changing the perception of that image is awkward. Perhaps their coupling is based more on habit than friendship.

The following pages deal with high-profile harmonist couples—people whose lives have been scrutinized over the years by a press that is flattering and merciless in turn. Harmonist women, often used to the public glare, are sometimes forced to live the worst moments of their relationships in the spotlight. It is not unknown for them to make damning statements about their partners in public. Disappointments run high. In real life the fairy tale can quickly run out of magic, except in the public's imagination.

*Some **harmonist women** work hard to stay attractive and the aging process may cause **great anxiety** within this group.*

Could the union with **Diana** ever have **worked** for Charles**?**

Charles and **Diana**

In 1980, upon the urging of the queen mother, Prince Charles agreed to meet Lady Diana Spencer, the teenage granddaughter of a family friend. Their encounter took place at the home of a polo-playing acquaintance, and as they chatted, seated on a hay bale, Diana talked about the death of Lord Mountbatten, Charles's uncle. The two had been exceedingly close, and Mountbatten's sudden demise the previous year, when his boat was blown up by an IRA bomb, had greatly saddened the prince.

Charles—by nature sensitive and idealistic—warmed to Diana during their sympathetic conversation, and from this meeting the relationship between the two developed. In 1981, the Prince of Wales announced his long-awaited engagement to Lady Diana Spencer, ending many years of speculation among the press and public about his choice of a bride.

Yet within three years of their marriage, Charles and Diana maintained separate bedrooms, public schedules, and private lives. Their divorce in 1996 was a sad postscript to the fairy-tale wedding. Though the shy and slightly frumpy teenager blossomed into one of the most glamorous women in the world, Camilla Parker Bowles in time proved to be the stronger love for Charles (see pp. 115–122).

The graph on the facing page shows how Charles and Diana's faces have the same mathematical proportions. The half of Diana's face on the left has the same number of squares as the half of Charles's face on the right. If each square were a note of music, they would be playing the same tune—a perfect visual harmony.

Observe the differences

The harmonism of Charles and Diana's faces is clearly seen above. But despite their harmonism, the shapes of their eyes and mouths (right) are entirely different.

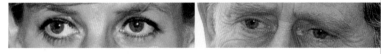

Diana's eyes   **Charles's eyes**

Diana's mouth   **Charles's mouth**

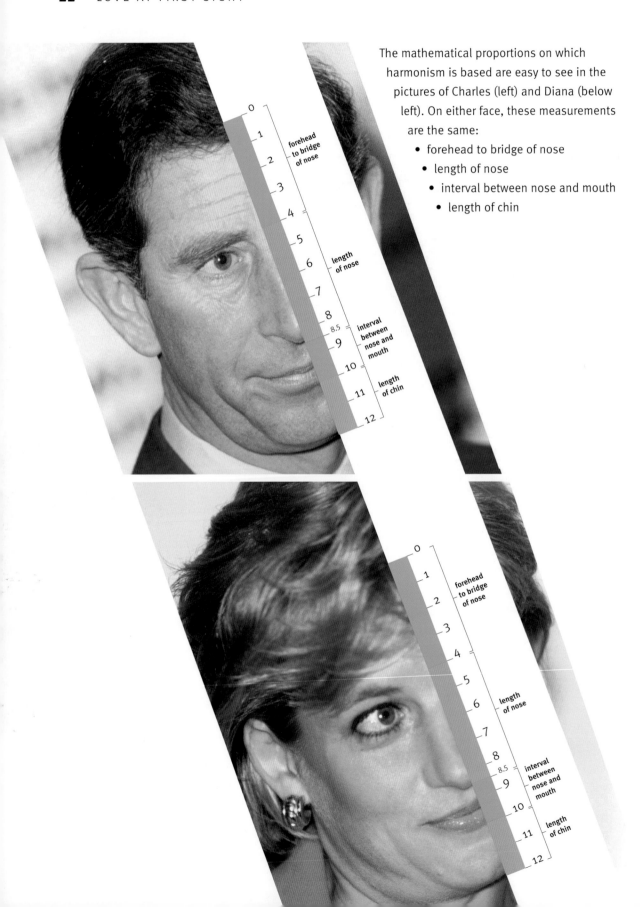

The mathematical proportions on which harmonism is based are easy to see in the pictures of Charles (left) and Diana (below left). On either face, these measurements are the same:

- forehead to bridge of nose
- length of nose
- interval between nose and mouth
- length of chin

0
1
2 forehead to bridge of nose
3
4
5
6 length of nose
7
8
8.5 interval between nose and mouth
9
10
11 length of chin
12

0
1
2 forehead to bridge of nose
3
4
5
6 length of nose
7
8
8.5 interval between nose and mouth
9
10
11 length of chin
12

The extent to which Charles and Diana's faces had a harmony both of proportion and expression can be seen in this picture, where the two halves of their respective faces seem to merge together as one.

In conclusion

Charles no doubt understood Diana's background of privilege and loneliness, and her sense of abandonment. Their childhood experiences may have been the common ground that brought them together, as well as their harmonist qualities. However, the same traits that may have attracted them to each other may also have been the source of their difficulties.

The hurt child in Diana needed healing. Depending on how great the injury, some partners are able to become "the healer." But Diana had suffered childhood pain that was too great perhaps for any person—even Charles—to resolve, especially since the hurt child in him also required comfort and support.

Charles and Diana were clearly each other's physical complement; their faces harmoniously wove into one, and they were physically attracted to one another. Had their emotional landscape been different, they might well have been happy together. We can only speculate. Certainly, none of Diana's other relationships, such as the one with James Hewitt (above), had such a propitious harmonist start.

Why **is there** so much harmonist **love** among actors **and** actresses**?**

Because they tend to have regularly proportioned faces, harmonists are often very attractive people. They frequently find their way into acting and are attracted to other people in that profession, and this may lead to marriage and lives lived in the glare of the world's media.

When beautiful people are attracted to each other this is often based on their harmonism.

Liz Hurley and **Hugh Grant**

In 1986, as an unknown young actor, Hugh Grant was offered the chance to film in Spain with another unknown—Elizabeth Hurley. It was to be the start of their relationship.

With the film *Four Weddings and a Funeral*, Hugh became a major player in Hollywood. At the première he was accompanied by Liz, who was wearing a Versace dress held together with designer safety pins. The attention she received for her fabulously good looks led to a contract (said to be worth $4.5m) with Estée Lauder—yet the following year Hugh was arrested for lewd conduct after he was caught with a prostitute, Divine Brown. He and Liz continued to live together for a while, but in June 2000 they split after a relationship of 13 years. Nevertheless, they remain close and Hugh is one of six godfathers to Liz's son, Damian.

Observe the differences

From the photographs above, it is clear to see that Hugh Grant and Liz Hurley do not resemble each other. They do not share the same shaped eyes or mouth (right).

Hugh's eyes　　　　　**Liz's eyes**

Hugh's mouth　　　　　**Liz's mouth**

scaling-up line

eye to nose

nose to lipline

lipline to edge of chin

The harmonist elements

Although their eyes and mouths are not the same shape, the illustrations above show the remarkable harmonism between Hugh and Liz. The horizontal lines show that they share similar distances between their main features, and the diagonal line slanting across each face grazes the edge of the nose and bisects the mouth at exactly the same angle. While two attractive people falling for each other is not unusual, in this case it was the result of their strong harmonism.

*After the initial **physical attraction** brings a harmonist couple together, the relationship will deepen when the **beauty** of the soul within is discovered.*

When they are seen from this angle, it is easily discernible that Liz and Hugh have the similar facial proportions that are found in harmonist couples.

In conclusion

After they split up, Hugh and Liz nevertheless acknowledged their value to each other. Although they spoke of their relationship as more akin to a brother-sister bond, in an interview with *Hello!* magazine in June 2000, Hugh said, "Liz stopped fancying me years ago."

The popular perception of what consistutes beauty is to a great extent shaped by the media and the image that is being promoted as the desirable one at the time. The importance of "inner beauty" is best demonstrated by the "beautiful people." There appears to be a very high attraction rate among these people, especially evendent in the worlds of theater and film, and a correspondingly high casualty rate. Initial attraction (harmonist) counts for much, but it is surely no substitute for discovering the beauty of the soul within.

Why **are harmonists** favorable partners with whom to have **children?**

Madonna and Guy Ritchie

Madonna Ciccone, born in 1958, was brought up in a working-class suburb of Bay City, Michigan. She has become the undisputed queen of the music industry since rising to prominence in 1984.

Guy Ritchie—10 years her junior—was educated at an elite private school, Stanbridge Earls, in the English county of Hampshire, and spent part of his youth at Loton Park, the 17th-century estate near Shrewsbury owned by his stepfather, Sir Michael Leighton. Guy is the director of the box-office hit films *Lock, Stock and Two Smoking Barrels* and *Snatch*.

The pair met at the Wiltshire estate of Sting and his wife, Trudie Styler, and a little over two years later were married in a very private ceremony at Skibo Castle in Scotland. Madonna has a daughter, Lourdes, from a previous relationship, and the couple now have a son, Rocco, born in August 2000.

Matching faces

Madonna and Guy have harmonism; their faces are in the same proportion. It is an aesthetic coupling. They like the way the other looks and, despite their very different ages and backgrounds, feel comfortable in each other's presence.

Although Madonna and Guy do not look alike, there are certain aspects of the eyes and mouth that appear similar when they smile. They have harmonism and—because of the similarities mentioned above—a small degree of echoism (see pp. 36–38). Their relationship therefore benefits from empathy and understanding, as well as their attraction to one another. Couples often do have the bonus of belonging to more than one visual love category.

The chin factor

Even when a person has found their harmonist, echoist, or prima copulist (see pp. 100–104) ideal, there are other visual considerations that may affect their happiness as a couple. The chin factor is the single most important element to influence the success or failure of a relationship because the chin contains information about the dominance or submissiveness of the person. The ideal partner is one who complements qualities lacking in the other.

When **both parties** in a relationship have strong, assertive chins, as can be seen in the photographs of **Madonna and Guy** (opposite), there is neither a **dominant** nor submissive partner.

The mouth and chin provide considerable information about a person's nature. Anger, meanness, and bitterness are the characteristics mirrored on the mouth, while strength and weakness are written on the chin.

This part of the face is not static and can change considerably during the course of an individual's life, depending upon their experiences and how they deal with them. The chin is not yet fully developed in young people, but if they become more forceful as they age, the chin will likewise become stronger. Conversely, if they grow weaker, that will also be reflected in the chin.

If a man with an exceptionally strong chin is in a partnership with a woman with a weak chin, he may be so dominant in the relationship that he overwhelms her. This dominant/submissive relationship may or may not suit both parties equally well (not all partners want to be equal).

When both partners in a relationship have strong, assertive chins, as can be seen in the photos of Guy and Madonna (opposite), there is not one dominant and one submissive partner: the "balance of power" is held equally. Such a couple may have to negotiate for dominance when it comes to deciding individual issues.

In conclusion

Behavioral studies with animals have shown that in the biologically driven search for a mate with good genes, it is the creatures that have a symmetrical appearance that are considered the most desirable.

This also occurs in the human race. Not only are harmonists good-looking people themselves, but they are also exercising an unconscious desire when mating to produce genetically strong offspring. Madonna and Guy have the harmonism that drives initial attraction and also some of the echoism that makes people begin to merge in their behavior. Their relationship becomes all the more fascinating when one considers their very different backgrounds and childhood experiences.

Echoi

sm

When a man or woman is attracted to their echoist match, there is a good chance that the attraction will be reciprocated because both parties will react to the easily recognizable similarities in their features.

What is an echoist?

An echoist looks like his or her partner, often to the extent that people who don't know them assume the pair to be members of the same family. Echoists have subconsciously recognized themselves in another person.

What is echoism?

The visual love category echoism is determined not by the proportions of the couple's faces (as in harmonism) but by three key shapes on the faces. These three shapes are that of the upper eyelid line, the upper lip line, and the sweep of the eyebrow. They will be of a comparable curve, line, or arch, and repeated in the face of either echoist partner, in effect producing a triple echo. The couple may have other features in common, but the size of the face and the coloring are not relevant.

The outer person reflects the inner being, and echoists are therefore often similar kinds of people. This is the love group of soulmates. Echoist couples are afforded the greatest luxury—that of being able to be themselves, without fear of judgment from the person with whom they share their life. They do not need to change their inner selves in order to accommodate their partner's requirements. Co-dependency is therefore not generally a feature of these relationships.

Because echoists are friends, they usually have a great deal of fun together. They see eye to eye on many levels and are likely to adopt each other's pursuits and interests.

It is often said that couples grow to look alike after they have been together for a long time. In the case of echoists, this popular idea is not entirely a fanciful one. They have looked alike right from the start, but that resemblance is not always immediately apparent. As people age, however, the degree of their likeness is emphasized. For example, a jutting lower lip will jut still more; heavy-lidded eyes will become heavier; deep-set eyes will sink farther into the face. Consequently, the similarities between the two people in an echoist relationship grow more evident with time. The couple may also begin the phenomenon of visual mirroring (see p. 43). Since this involves the use of identical muscles of the face, they will resemble each other even more as lines and creases start to form.

There is also a strong likelihood that during their partnership they will share many activities together, and this can affect their appearance. A couple who enjoy sailing, for example, will develop similarly weather-beaten faces; vacationing in exotic locations together, they will share the effects of exposure to the sun. But despite the effects of time and tide, their companionship should lead to aging together comfortably.

When the first flush of passion fades, the echoist couple still have their friendship and a certain understanding. They often tolerate more from each other than people in non-echoist relationships because they have empathy with each other.

Echoism is simply the starting point of attraction, the common ground before other factors are involved. As with all relationships, personality and the meeting of emotional needs have their own part to play.

*The **outer person** reflects the **inner being**, and echoists therefore tend to be **similar** kinds of people. This is the love group of **soulmates**.*

Generally speaking, echoist couples try hard not to hurt one another if for some reason their partnership does not last. They tend not to bring each other's faults into the public arena for discussion, criticism, and comment. They are partners. The 20th-century French dramatist Jean Anouilh commented that being in love is a way of loving oneself. This saying is never more true than in the love of the echoist couple.

Couples in this visual love category appear to have a remarkable ability to surmount the problems posed by coming from different races, backgrounds, or generations. Their mutual echoist understanding can bridge the gap caused by disparities in color, class, or age. However, if the cultural and social boundaries are not those that both partners wish to cross, no amount of echoism will help. Echoist couples often share the same interest or ideology, and there are many fascinating examples of echoist couples in this section of the book.

The heavy price that echoists pay for their fulfilling relationship is the terrible sense of loss that comes with bereavement. During a long and happy partnership each of the pair fills the position of mate and best friend. The grief of the surviving echoist partner is compounded by the loss of their dearest friend at the time when they are most needed.

People **in love** have a special presence: why does **all** the **world** love a **lover?**

Victoria and **David Beckham**

Victoria Beckham, also known as "Posh," was formerly a member of the Spice Girls pop group; David Beckham, also known as "Becks," is a talented soccer player and role model for many young people. What Posh and Becks do as individuals may hit the headlines, but it is their relationship that is the biggest news.

David Beckham met Victoria Adams in 1997. Ten months later, in January 1998, they became engaged, with Victoria telling *OK!* magazine, "I am the happiest girl in the world." The fairy-tale wedding that ensued was eagerly anticipated by the world's media, which since then has followed their every move. Posh and Becks have two sons, Brooklyn and Romeo.

Observe the similarities

- forehead with a pronounced widow's peak
- similarly shaped brows
- inner corners of the eyes are slightly pulled down
- neat nostrils
- no deep fleshy creases or lines between nose and mouth
- curvaceous, clearly defined upper lip
- corners of mouth when smiling look like half commas
- lower lips rounded and full
- neat, elfin-shaped chin

One sign of advancing age is the deepening creases that manifest themselves between the nose and mouth. David and Victoria have a shared characteristic flatness around this area, and in their faces the aging process will show mainly elsewhere. David and Victoria may look increasingly alike since their signs of aging will no doubt be similar if they continue to use the same facial muscles as they mirror one another.

Not only do David and Victoria have the echoism that allows them to see eye to eye, but they also have harmonism, which means that their faces are mathematically of the same proportion. People in a harmonist relationship look "right" together.

Victoria and David look good as a couple but they also are good together because—being an echoist couple—they are good friends. In this case their glamour, looks, and careers serve to sustain public interest in their relationship.

Truly love at first sight

When David first saw Victoria on a Spice Girls video, he had no idea that her face was in the same proportion as his own, or that her eyes and mouth were the same shape as his. He did not perceive her as a reflection of himself; he just saw Victoria and fell in love.

However, his subconscious instantly took in their mathematical match. The magnetic pull that drew David to Victoria while watching the pop video was the recognition of self in another person. That moment of instant recognition is "love at first sight."

About pheromones

These are chemicals produced by the body that are important in awakening sexual desire, but they have no significance when it comes to the phenomenon of falling in love at first sight. It is possible to fall in love through the screen or by seeing a photograph where smell and touch are not factors. At this moment an individual has no idea if the object of their love will smell or feel "right." Visually, a person knows that they have found their love match.

The visual process forms a large part of the way a man loves. For men, it is visual attraction that creates the initial relationship; for women, the relationship can create an attraction that was not there at the beginning. Generally speaking, it is unlikely that a man will ever fall in love with a woman he does not find visually attractive, even though she may be attracted to him.

*Wholeheartedly embracing their **celebrity status**, and blessed **with love** and mutual respect, Posh and Becks have apparently **conquered** their world.*

Visual mirroring

"Mirroring" occurs when a couple are so close that they copy each other's facial expressions. It is a deeply unconscious compliment each partner pays the other, and it can be seen in these pictures of Victoria and David Beckham.

"I don't know where I begin and he ends," is the remark that often accompanies mirroring. The couple are unaware that they are borrowing the expressions of the loved one, of course, since they cannot see their own faces. This mirroring will then be copied by their children so that the characteristic becomes part of the family "look."

Sometimes a child does not resemble either parent, but if the parents are very close-knit the child will mirror their shared expressions and so look like part of the family. This explains how a child who is adopted by mirroring partners can grow to resemble them.

In conclusion

All the world loves a lover because human beings are fascinated by the mystery of real love—especially if it appears to endure. As a couple, Victoria and David Beckham have taken on the status of new royalty, with a romance that is more satisfying than the union of Prince Charles and Diana Spencer. This is one fairy tale that seems true.

We want to believe that it is possible to have it all: beauty, talent, money, fame, and love. As long as they adore each other the magic of Posh and Becks will persist. In effect, their love, which has played out on a world stage, has significantly boosted their public profiles and careers.

The recipients of celebrity and money are often isolated by these attributes to the extent that they become victims. David and Victoria Beckham are not victims. They are in control. Wholeheartedly embracing their celebrity status, and blessed with love and mutual respect, Posh and Becks have apparently conquered their world.

This love has fueled an industry. A photograph of Posh and Becks on the front page of a tabloid newspaper or a magazine can produce the skyrocketing sales that once accompanied a story about Princess Diana. Why do sales soar? Do people want to learn their thoughts or views? No. They simply want to know the secret of their love.

Does all **echoist love** burn with equal **intensity** or can a **cool coupling** work just as well**?**

Edward and **Sophie Wessex**

This echoist match is rather different from that of Victoria and David Beckham. In January 1999, Prince Edward, the youngest son of Queen Elizabeth II, announced his engagement to Sophie Rhys-Jones after a five-year courtship. To the outside world it looked like a cool kind of love—but not everyone yearns to love on a higher plane where, as David Beckham is reported to have said, the nature of the love is so intense that it hurts.

Observe the similarities

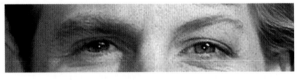

Edward's eye   **Sophie's eye**

The shapes of the eyebrow, upper eyelid line, and
upper lip line are echoed in both faces.

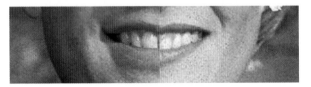

Edward's mouth   **Sophie's mouth**

*An outwardly **cool marriage** may have strong foundations and therefore outlast unions that are **passionate** and intense.*

An empathetic love

There are varying degrees of echoist love, from friendship and platonic love to intense romance. Of course, it is not possible to know what is in another person's heart, but with echoism you can read the clues in a partner's face.

After their protracted courtship, Sophie and Edward were finally married in 1999. Shortly after the wedding, Sophie announced to the press that she would be spending only the weekends with Edward at their country retreat. Weekdays would be spent separately so that Edward "could adjust to his marital state after bachelorhood." Just a few years after their wedding, Edward was reportedly very angry when, on a visit abroad, separate rooms had not been booked for them.

It is an outwardly cool coupling, yet one that is built on firm foundations. The photographs below show the remarkably similar facial vocabulary of Sophie and Edward: the shapes of the eyebrow, upper eyelid line, and upper lip line are all the same. Theirs is an echoist partnership, and they have the strong friendship that is typical of echoism. They also have harmonism: Sophie's nose is a little longer than Edward's, but otherwise their faces are in almost the same proportions. This strong base provides an empathy for one another and a special understanding.

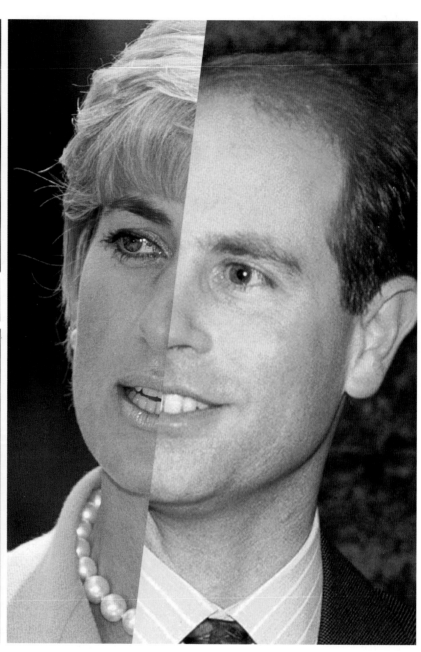

Sisters-in-law

The similarity in appearance between sisters-in-law Princess Diana and Sophie Wessex is often remarked upon. Is there a reason why Charles's wife looked like Edward's? Could Edward have been as attracted to Diana as he is to Sophie?

Edward and Diana (above) have the same facial proportions—they have harmonism—but they do not have echoism. Edward and Sophie have harmonism and echoism: they have the same shaped eyebrows, upper eyelid line, and upper lip line. On its own, a harmonist attraction to a sister-in-law probably will not run deep.

Sophie and Diana (above) have harmonism. They do not have echoism (the shape of the eyebrows, upper eyelid line, and upper lip line are not the same), but their shared harmonism gives them a certain similarity. When brothers have similar facial proportions and each takes a harmonist partner, the sisters-in-law may well look alike.

*Married to brothers with **the same facial proportions**, sisters-in-law may well share a **visual** similarity.*

In conclusion

When brothers have the same facial proportions, if one of them marries their harmonist match the brother may also find his new sister-in-law attractive. The attraction probably will not run deep unless the brother and sister-in-law share the same shapes of facial features (echoism). Sisters-in-law may often bear a resemblance to each other when the brothers have the same facial proportions.

It is not uncommon for two brothers to marry two sisters. Elvis's father Vernon Presley married Gladys, who was part Cherokee. Vernon's brother Lester married Clettes, Gladys's sister. Napoleon's brother Joseph married Julie Clary. Napoleon was poised to marry Désirée, sister of Julie, suggesting that this relationship may have had the harmonist characteristics of two brothers who were attracted to two sisters. Napoleon might even have married Désirée, had he not met his prima copulist love Josephine (pp. 133–138).

Returning to Sophie and Edward, we have seen that their relationship is both echoist and harmonist. Generally, if echoist partnerships come unstuck, the couple remain friends. No friendship remained after the split of Edward's older brother Charles with his harmonist partner Diana, unlike the harmonist-echoist marriage and divorce of middle brother Prince Andrew and Sarah Ferguson(pp. 57–60).

What led two **brothers** from a **distinguished** American family to pursue the **same woman?**

Marilyn Monroe and **John F. Kennedy**

The distinguished family was the Kennedys. The two brothers were John F. Kennedy (Jack) and his brother Robert. The woman in question was screen goddess Marilyn Monroe.

Marilyn's affair with Jack spanned a decade. It was terminated after she famously serenaded "Mr. President" in Madison Square Garden on his 45th birthday. What she did was so provocative that Broadway columnist Dorothy Kilgallen described her as "making love to the president in the direct view of 40 million Americans."

Marilyn was a friend of Frank Sinatra, who had a connection with Mafia boss Sam Giancana. The latter wanted to have markers on the president (people who could pass on information about his movements), so the relationship with Marilyn was a matter of considerable concern not only to the White House but also to the FBI and CIA.

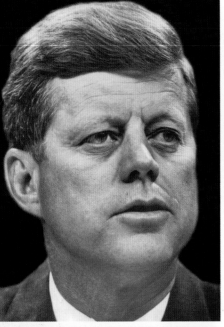

Beyond the physical

When a woman has both echoism and harmonism with a man, she often feels that she has found a friend as well as a lover. Marilyn had both with Jack (p. 54). She revealed to her friend Bob Slatzer that Kennedy had told her they would be man and wife one day. For her this was more than an affair.

Jack and his younger brother Robert had been groomed for political life since they were born; they were trained to put their career ambitions before any other needs or desires. Marilyn was the emotionally needy "orphan number 3463" from the Los Angeles Orphan Home. It is hardly surprising that she was not able to put her own career ambitions before an affair of the heart.

The relationship between Jack and Marilyn may have appeared purely sexual, but some of the Kennedy family thought otherwise. Jack's brother-in-law Peter Lawford, who had introduced the two in 1950 and at whose house they frequently met, said that of all Jack's women, Marilyn was the one who complemented him most. They had a sense of humor that clicked.

*Peter Lawford, **Jack's brother-in-law**, said that of all Jack's women, Marilyn **complemented him most**. They had a sense of humor **that clicked**.*

Observe the similarities

Marilyn and Jack had both harmonism and echoism:

- similar facial proportions
- same wide mouth
- similar upper lip shape (Marilyn's lip shape was often distorted by lipstick)

- similar curve of lower lip
- same base of nose and nostril shape
- similarly almond-shaped eyes (The puffiness around Jack's eyes was a result of the drugs he took for Addison's disease and his chronic back problems.)

*Marilyn had **harmonism** with Robert but **echoism** and **harmonism** with Jack. Thus her bond with **Jack** was probably the stronger one.*

Robert Kennedy, Jack's younger brother, is said to have become involved with Marilyn when he went to see her—on his brother's behalf —to put an end to Marilyn's relationship with Jack. Marilyn's affair with Robert lasted a mere six months. According to some reports, it finished when Marilyn, who had yearned for a baby all her life, underwent an abortion in July 1962. Following this Robert's ardor cooled, and he terminated their relationship.

More than two hundred books about Marilyn have appeared since her death. Whatever may be gleaned from them about her relationships with Jack and Robert Kennedy, the information on their three faces tells us that her relationship with Jack was stronger than that with Robert. With Robert she had only harmonism: attraction was there but it did not run deep. With Jack she had echoism as well. The abrupt loss of the echoist lover with whom she also "clicked" was hard for Marilyn.

In conclusion

Fifteen days after the abortion, on Saturday, August 4, 1962, Marilyn was found dead in Los Angeles from what appeared to be a drug overdose. She was just 36 years old. Although suicide was supposed, rumors abounded that Marilyn had been killed to silence her and thus protect the Kennedy family name.

Marilyn was subject to mood swings and had attempted suicide several times. At the time of her death she was being treated by a psychiatrist for her dependence on Nembutal (pentobarbital sodium)—a sedative and hypnotic drug that she used to help her sleep. It is possible that her death was accidental, caused by a cocktail of this and other drugs or alcohol.

There are numerous conspiracy theories that point to FBI or Mafia involvement in Marilyn's demise; none has been proved. But this much can be said: had she not become so famously embroiled with Jack and Robert Kennedy, the circumstances surrounding her death would not remain open to question.

Why do **Andrew** and **Fergie** remain **such** good friends?

Prince Andrew and Sarah Ferguson

Prince Andrew, the second son of Queen Elizabeth II, met Sarah Ferguson (later nicknamed "Fergie" by the press) at a house party during Royal Ascot week in 1985. When they married the following year, Sarah became Duchess of York. Andrew and Sarah divorced in 1998.

Despite the trials and tribulations of Sarah's much-publicized life after the divorce, the couple remain friends. The emotional bond that they established continues to this day. Following the divorce, Sarah lived on in the marital home—Sunninghill Park, provided by the queen—for some years. The couple remain good friends and still take vacations together with their children several times a year.

Observe the similarities

The pictures above and opposite provide clues to the bond that unites Andrew and Sarah.

HARMONIST FEATURES

- same long forehead
- same length nose
- same distance between nose and mouth
- same heavy and wide jawline
- same long squareish chin

ECHOIST FEATURES

- same arched eyebrows
- same eye shape
- same thin mouth
- same upper lip

They have other echoist and harmonist features too. Their mouths and eyes are similarly shaped, and the distances between these features are in the same proportion. The lower eyelid line is straight, so that their expressions often register as merriment or surprise in the same way. When they smile, the upper lip almost disappears.

Andrew and Sarah have harmonism: they like the way each other looks and feel comfortable together. And they have echoism: they look like each other, recognize themselves in each other, and have the friendship that is characteristic of echoist couples. It is these factors that continue to bind them closely together.

Friendship is key to an *echoist couple. On the day their divorce became final, Sarah told the press, "Andrew is my bestest friend."*

In conclusion

Echoism is simply the starting point of attraction: at its heart, an echoist relationship is based on love, mutual understanding, and kinship. When the first flush of ardor dies down, echoists are fortunate enough to have this strong base to their relationship. In royal circles—as in all walks of life—true friendship is something to treasure.

If Andrew and Sarah go on spending time together, their facial similarities will probably increase as they reflect and mirror one another (please read page 43 for an explanation of visual mirroring). With their shared harmonism and echoism, complete separation would be difficult for both of them.

The two studies on second marriages (pp. 92–99) suggest that when people choose to marry again, the second partner is often similar to the first, either physically or in their behavioral type. It is like repeating a language that has been learned and loved. If Andrew does decide to marry again, it is probable that he will choose a woman who is the same strong and courageous type as Sarah.

What was the **source** of Margaret Thatcher's **strength** and **confidence?**

Margaret and Denis Thatcher

At the height of their success, the Spice Girls pop group had what was known as "girl power." Victoria Beckham—Posh Spice—once called Margaret Thatcher "the first Spice Girl." Perhaps Posh thought that the "girl power" they shared came from the same source. Both women have enjoyed the unconditional love of a strong, supportive echoist partner.

Margaret Thatcher, a grocer's daughter from Grantham in Lancashire, England, achieved academic distinction at Oxford University and worked as a research chemist while pursuing her political ambitions. She married Denis Thatcher in 1950, was elected Conservative member of Parliament for Finchley in the 1959 general election, and in 1970 became secretary of state for education and science. On May 4, 1979, Margaret Thatcher became Britain's first female prime minister.

Strong partners

In her autobiography *The Path to Power*, Margaret Thatcher described the opposition she received as secretary of state for education and science.

She felt that a woman in a man's world is more vulnerable to personal abuse than a man is. "But any politician who wants to hold high office must be prepared to go through something like this," she wrote. "Some are broken by it, others strengthened. Denis, as always the essence of commonsense, came through magnificently. If I survived it was due to his love and support."

Margaret Thatcher went on to be leader of the Conservative Party for 15 years and prime minister for nearly 12. The part Denis played as her physical and emotional complement cannot be underestimated.

Echoist love is ideal when forging a career. An **echoist partner** will provide **not just love** but also understanding and support to the **aspiring partner**.

Strong profiles, strong partners: Margaret Thatcher attributed her outstanding success to the support of her husband Denis, who gave her a shining confidence.

In conclusion

Echoist love is ideal when forging a career. An echoist partner will provide love, understanding, and support to the aspiring partner. Echoists are less inclined to be envious of their partner's success, and more likely to bask in reflected glory. Margaret Thatcher was loved unconditionally by a strong echoist partner, and described Denis as the "golden thread" running through her life.

Power needs a backbone, and the strongest backbone is to be genuinely loved. Margaret, known as the Iron Lady, had armor reinforced with love, the strongest mettle. Typical in his echoist support, Denis never expressed the slightest degree of irritation that he appeared to play second fiddle to his wife. Quite the contrary: when asked who wore the pants in the relationship, he joked that he did, and that he washed and ironed them too.

Mikhail and Raisa Gorbachev

The more "traditional" pairing of a woman behind a powerful man is found in the marriage of the Gorbachevs. Mikhail Gorbachev, former president of the USSR, studied at Moscow State University as a young man. At the student club, he met Raisa Maksimova. In his autobiography *Memoirs,* he wrote, "Little did I know that I went to meet my destiny. From that day on, there began for me a period of torment and delight."

Even when Raisa and Mikhail were married they had to live separately in female and male student quarters where access to zones was strictly regulated by a system of permits. Great effort was required on Mikhail's part to obtain authorization for daily visits to his wife, during which he had to carry his passport as proof that his marriage was legal. But even this was of no avail when, at exactly 11 o'clock each night, the telephone would ring in Raisa's room and the concierge on duty would say, "An unauthorized person is in your room."

Fortunately, the enforced separation did not have a long-term effect on his marriage to his echoist wife Raisa, with whom he fulfilled a glittering political career. It is generally thought by many Russians that Raisa did not simply support her husband but often initiated policy and had a powerful influence on the decisions he made in the political arena.

The three photographs below show the echoist elements of Mikhail and Raisa Gorbachev's faces. They shared the same-shaped eyebrows, the same slant of the upper eyelid, a similarly rounded base to the nose, with deep creases at the sides, and similarly shaped chins.

Václav Havel and Dagmar Veskrnova

Václav Havel was born into a privileged Czech family whose members included architects, filmmakers, and diplomats. Havel himself was best known abroad as a poet and playwright before he became president of Czechoslovakia on December 29, 1989.

Havel swept to power on a wave of popular support that was also extended to his wife, Olga. The couple had married in 1964, and Havel referred to her as his indispensable source of support. After Havel was elected president, Olga undertook charitable work that won her awards internationally. She was extremely popular with the Czech public and after her death from cancer in January 1996 they turned out in their thousands to pay their respects at Prague Castle.

Consequently, when Havel married actress Dagmar Veskrnova less than a year later his public standing was badly dented. Not only was the marriage too soon, but Dagmar's career had also included a role as a topless vampire. But Havel was not deterred, for in Dagmar he has met his echoist match. They share a characteristic smile, broad and impish, with similarly curved lips. There is also strong resemblance around the eyes and the base of the nose.

How did a 14-year-old schoolgirl win a famous soldier's heart?

Elvis and Priscilla Presley

In 1958, Priscilla Beaulieu, daughter of an American military family stationed in Germany, went to an American army camp in Wiesbaden, where she was introduced to a soldier. He was not just any soldier: he was Elvis Presley, an internationally acclaimed star—the king of rock 'n' roll—and he was completing his military service. Priscilla was 14 years old and a freshman in high school. A strange courtship ensued.

Elvis returned to civilian life in the US, and Priscilla visited him briefly, but afterward Elvis felt unable to live without his "baby." He begged Priscilla's stepfather, Colonel Beaulieu, to allow her to leave Germany and live at Graceland, the Presley family home in Memphis, Tennessee, promising that she would receive a good Catholic education and would graduate from high school. Colonel Beaulieu was won over, and Priscilla went to live with Elvis, his grandmother, his father Vernon, and the ever-present entourage of "guys" who surrounded the music star.

In the cloistered environment of Graceland, night had become day. On her first day there Priscilla learned to take amphetamines in order to keep the same late-night hours as Elvis, who woke only in the late afternoon. Graceland lived by its own rules, imposed by "the King."

Strange days at Graceland

At Graceland, the outside world was regarded with scorn. The guys who attached themselves to Elvis, resentful of Priscilla's intrusion, vied for his attention and favors. Elvis wanted to show the guys that a woman could not control him and was determined to demonstrate that he was still in charge.

Priscilla quickly learned her place. Elvis was training her to be the kind of woman he wanted. She discovered that she had to keep her mouth shut and pay attention to everything the King said, approving of his behavior and laughing at the appropriate time.

Priscilla remained at Graceland with Elvis's father and grandmother, attending school but hopelessly bored the rest of the time. Meanwhile, Elvis was often absent, involved in movies and his affairs with women. Throughout this time the couple frequently slept in the same bed, but Elvis was adamant that Priscilla remain "pure." He said that he did not wish to jeopardize their future together by having intercourse before they were married—that there would be a right time and place for it and that when the time came (Elvis assured Priscilla), he would know it.

Although Priscilla was subordinate to the King, Elvis for his part was controlled by his manager, "Colonel" Parker. His "interference" prevented Elvis and Priscilla's relationship from following its natural course. The Colonel not only told Elvis who he could marry, but also when.

One day in 1967, eight years after they first met, Elvis went down on his knees before Priscilla. Presenting her with a ring, he told her that the time was now right. But the pattern established during their courtship continued after the wedding. Elvis maintained his affairs during long absences from home, and the lack of privacy continued in their enclosed, day-into-night marriage. Moreover, the sexual abstinence maintained during their eight-year courtship was reestablished after the birth of their daughter, Lisa Marie, in 1968, when Elvis declared that women are no longer desirable after they have had a baby.

Christmas 1971 Priscilla announced that she was leaving Elvis. Only then did he become aware of how much he had lost. He had fallen in love with Priscilla at first sight, and had remarked particularly upon the bone structure of her face. It was, of course, similar to his own.

*Meeting **Priscilla** for the first time, **Elvis remarked** particularly upon **the bone structure** of her face. It was, of course, similar to **his own**.*

Losing Priscilla was the second major blow in Elvis's life (the first was when his mother died). The divorce decree was granted on October 9, 1973, at the Los Angeles County Courthouse. The couple held hands with each other throughout the proceedings. When Priscilla looked back at Elvis at the moment of their departure from the courthouse, he winked at her. Within the week, the King—now seriously dependent on drugs—was admitted to hospital in a semicomatose condition. Following his release, he needed 10 weeks of recuperation.

In conclusion

Elvis and Priscilla were a good echoist match, but there were many factors that made it impossible for them to enjoy it and develop their relationship into a successful, lasting union. Fame, fans, and hangers-on ultimately spoiled the King. An adoring Priscilla, unable to handle the situation, was forced to subdue her true nature.

The balance of power established during their courtship weighted the relationship too strongly in Elvis's favor. This meant that the subdued Priscilla could not be the real friend to him that he needed. The fact that they held hands in the courtroom during their divorce proceedings is a testament to the depth of the echoist love and friendship that Elvis had sadly neglected during their marriage.

Do the principles of **echoism** apply to **people** of all kinds**?**

Emperor Akihito and **Empress Michiko**

John Lennon and **Yoko Ono**

Henry Dent-Brocklehurst and **Lili Maltese**

Phil Collins and **Orianne Cevey**

Prince Constantijn of the Netherlands and **Laurentien**

Steffi Graf and **Andre Agassi**

Brad Pitt and **Jennifer Aniston**

Frankie and **Catherine Dettori**

Melanie Griffiths and **Antonio Banderas**

Ulrika and **Lance Gerrard-Wright**

Noah and **Tracy Wyle**

Charlie and **Oona Chaplin**

Mickey and **January Rooney**

Bob and **Dolores Hope**

Emperor Akihito and Empress Michiko

Emperor Akihito of Japan married Michiko against fierce opposition from his mother and the Imperial Household Agency. She was the first commoner to enter the Japanese Imperial family. The strong echoism between them is seen in the three key shapes of the eyebrow, upper eyelid line, and upper lip line.

After their son, Crown Prince Naruhito, followed in his father's footsteps by marrying a commoner (pp. 150–151), the Imperial Household Agency began leaking stories to the media claiming that Empress Michiko was not worthy of her exalted position. As a result, she suffered a period of depression followed by a minor stroke and this left her unable to speak for seven months. The outraged Japanese public forced the media to withdraw their stories, and two of the offending magazine publishers were almost assassinated by those who felt that the empress had been deeply wronged.

It was perhaps inevitable that Akihito would be determined to marry Michiko: the echoism they share is so strong. Has the match come at a high price for Michiko's health? The antagonism she endured may have contributed to the nervous breakdown she suffered early in her marriage.

John Lennon and Yoko Ono

People can find their echoist (or harmonist) match even when they come from different races. John Lennon was born in the English port of Liverpool, Yoko Ono in Tokyo, Japan. They had echoism, and their loving relationship made it possible for them to further both their political and creative ideals.

When John Lennon met Yoko Ono in 1966, they were both still married to other people, although Yoko had separated from her husband two years earlier. They made their romance publicly known in 1968, and the next year held a secret wedding in Gibraltar followed by a very public "bed-in" at Amsterdam's Hilton hotel. "Stay in bed, grow your hair," was the couple's anti-violence, anti-war, pro-love message. They wanted the whole world to know and follow their love example.

Henry Dent-Brocklehurst and Lili Maltese

British aristocrat Henry Dent-Brocklehurst is the custodian of 12th-century Sudeley Castle in Gloucestershire, England. Lili Maltese is a Hawaiian-born model who grew up on the island of Maui. Although their genetic, cultural, and social backgrounds are different, they have formed an echoist match. There is a similarity in their eyes, and a strong resemblance in the shape of the mouth and set of the teeth.

Phil Collins and Orianne Cevey

An echoist match knows no barriers. Swiss interpreter Orianne Cevey is the third wife of English musician Phil Collins and 22 years his junior. In this pair, the sweep of the eyebrow and shape of the upper eyelid line are the same.

Prince Constantijn and Laurentien

A good example of echoism can be seen in the case of Prince Constantijn of the Netherlands and his bride Laurentien Brinkhorst: her distinctive mouth and teeth echo those of her groom. Laurentien is a commoner. Many Dutch mothers may have wondered why their attractive (and perhaps more eligible) daughters were passed over in favor of the woman to whom the prince is no doubt devoted.

Steffi Graf and Andre Agassi

Sports personalities are subject to intense competition and its consequent stress. Away from the glamour, training is demanding and being a "sports partner" needs an understanding of these rigors. Often, echoist love provides the empathy required to sustain such a relationship.

Tennis champion Andre Agassi was once married to model and actress Brooke Shields. Brooke's career had begun when she was chosen, aged 11 months, as the Ivory Snow Baby. Strange then that Andre allegedly stuck a picture of Steffi Graf on the refrigerator door to inspire his wife to stay in shape. The marriage lasted only two years.

Andre said of Steffi that he had always adored and admired her from afar, remarking that he is strong willed and persistent when focused. He pursued Steffi and the couple were married in October 2001, a few days before the birth of their son Jaden Gil.

Observe the similarities between the shapes of their main features (below and opposite). It is easy to see that Steffi and Andre have echoism. Often, the similarity between two people does not become clear until they have children. First, the child appears to be the image of the mother and then one sees the likeness to the father.

This is because during the early years of physical development, the child of an echoist couple will display the visual characteristics of both parents. The similarity between the two parents may not be clear until the child's likeness to both shows that theirs is an echoist match.

Observe the similarities

Andre's eye
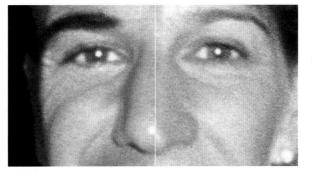
Steffi's eye

- same-shaped eyebrows, curving on the temples
- same-shaped eyes

- eyes seem to peer in the same way
- similar long-spined noses
- similar shape at the base of the noses

Brad Pitt and Jennifer Aniston

Brad Pitt is an acclaimed Hollywood actor, once dubbed "sexiest man alive." Jennifer Aniston rose to fame in the popular TV sitcom *Friends*. The pair began dating in the summer of 1998.

They were serious about each other right from the start. Brad said that Jennifer was the one and only; Jennifer described their romance as the happiest time of her life. They were married in July 2000 in Malibu, taking their vows on a cliff top at sunset under a bamboo arch. On the eve of their third wedding anniversary in July 2003, Brad told *Hello!* magazine, "You have to find someone you can truly be yourself with," which simply defines the essence of echoism. On the

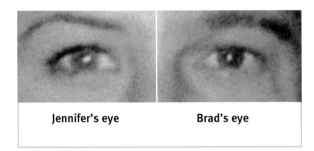

| Jennifer's eye | Brad's eye |

same occasion, Jennifer said, "I think it has made me more comfortable in who I am to have someone who loves me and accepts me with all my dysfunction and insecurities and struggles."

Brad said, "You have to find someone you can *truly* be yourself with." *Echoist couples are afforded **the greatest** luxury—that of being able **to be** themselves.*

Frankie and Catherine Dettori

In 1996, Frankie Dettori was the first jockey to ride seven winners in seven races at Ascot, thereby cementing his reputation as one of the greatest riders of all time. He was born in Milan to a father who was a top Italian jockey and a circus-artist mother whose act included horseback stunts.

At the age of 14 Frankie arrived in England, where an apprenticeship to a racehorse trainer at Newmarket set him on his path to his triumphs. His wife, Cambridge-educated Catherine Allen, is the daughter of a New Zealand-born professor who is a pioneer in horse-breeding techniques. The couple were married in 1997 and now have three children—all born during race meetings.

While the world of horse-racing brought the couple together, they are otherwise from different backgrounds, both geographically and culturally. However, their union is bound by echoism and a certain amount of harmonism. The shape of their eyes and the sweep of their brows are similar, as are the distances between their main features.

Melanie Griffiths and Antonio Banderas

Melanie Griffiths has all-American good looks and Antonio Banderas is the archetypal Latin lover. It might therefore seem unlikely that echoism brought them together. On close examination, however, they can be seen to be echoists: note their upper eyelid lines and the sweep of their eyebrows, as well as the similar shape to their lips and the identical expressions on their mouths.

Ulrika and Lance Gerrard-Wright

Ulrika Jonsson met Lance Gerrard-Wright when she was hosting the British TV show *Mr. Right*, which had been designed to find him a suitable partner from among 15 women. Lance may already have had an attraction to Ulrika: her face was familiar to him from viewing *Shooting Stars*, one of his favorite programs.

Ulrika may have helped to select Lance for the show because she was already attracted to him. In July 2003, shortly before their wedding, she told *OK!* magazine that when she first saw a picture of him "he seemed to look too nice and clean cut," but that after she met him she felt the show should be retitled *Mr. Perfect*. Ulrika and Lance are an echoist match, and it follows a classic echoist pattern in that they describe each other as soulmates and friends. Ulrika has even decided to abandon the maiden name by which she is better known in favor of his last name.

Noah and Tracy Wyle

Star of the hospital drama series *ER*, Noah Wyle met his future wife Tracy on the set of *The Myth of Fingerprints*. Noah was attracted to Tracy, a makeup artist three years his senior, right from the start. He is reported to have said that he always knew where they would end up.

Their likeness is not just in the shape of their features, but also in how they use them. They have a similar expression around the mouth. Noah and Tracy were married in May 2000.

Charlie and Oona Chaplin

An age gap of several decades can often be successfully bridged when the couple have echoism. Echoists are friends and may be soulmates.

Charlie Chaplin, the much-loved actor and film director, married Oona O'Neill when she was 18 and he was 54. Despite the difference in their ages, the couple lived a happy life together until Charlie's death at the age of 88. Observe the similarities: the shape of the eyes, heavy eyebrows set close to them, and the high cheekbones.

Mickey and January Rooney

Considering the 33-year age gap between the couple, observers may have viewed actor Mickey Rooney's eighth marriage with scepticism.

His track record of seven previous marriages (one lasted a mere 100 days) did not bode well for a long future together. Mickey was 58 when he took January Chamberlin, a 25-year-old singer-composer, as his bride. Their facial similarities are so pronounced that the couple could easily pass for father and daughter. Could this have helped them notch up 25 years together?

Bob and Dolores Hope

Celebrity unions that endure for years are often found in the echoist visual love category. The marriage of Bob Hope and nightclub singer Dolores Reade is one example. Their wedding took place on February 19, 1934, in Erie, Pennsylvania, and their marriage, with its ups and downs, lasted almost 70 years.

The facial similarities of Bob and Dolores—in particular their wide mouths and firm line of the jaw—are evident in the photographs above, taken in their younger years. The likeness is even more pronounced (see below) after a lifetime of visual mirroring. This phenomenon occurs when a couple are so close that they unconsciously copy each other's facial expressions.

In conclusion

Although many of the people featured in this section are conventionally good-looking, one certainly need not be beautiful to find echoist love. Good looks are not relevant when finding one's echoist match. In fact, the more unusual a feature a person may have, the greater the chance that it will attract a mate with a similar idiosyncracy.

Echoist love crosses many divides and can surmount the apparent obstacles of social, cultural, age, and geographical differences (as can be seen from the examples in this section) if both partners so wish. Despite this, an understanding of and empathy for a partner are basic and necessary requirements of enduring echoist love, and indeed of love in any of the visual love categories.

Other factors can determine the success (or failure) of a love relationship. Family history and individual life experience can have an enormous impact on a person's character and emotional nature, and are often significant in establishing the role either partner plays in the relationship. The ideal partner is one who complements the other, and here too roles are played out—the healer and the healed, the mentor and the life student, and so on. Sexual chemistry can seem a powerful bond at first—but stripped of emotion fulfills nothing more than the basic desire of the human race to reproduce itself. How many satisfying and enduring relationships have started with the "one-night stand"? It is driven only by animal instinct, and highlights the need for other factors to mesh before a relationship is cemented.

Character, personality, intellect, and sexual attraction (which ultimately may wane) all have important roles to play in finding one's love match. It is when they are combined with one of the visual love categories—harmonism, echoism, or prima copulism—that a relationship will stand a greater chance of success.

Is there a **downside** to a happy **echoist** partnership**?**

Paula Yates and **Michael Hutchence**

Paul and **Linda McCartney**

Paul McCartney and **Heather Mills**

An echoist partnership can bring the greatest happiness, but the price it exacts is the terrible sense of loss that comes with bereavement. The grief of the surviving partner is compounded by the loss of their dearest friend at the time when they are most needed.

Paula Yates and Michael Hutchence

Paula Yates was the fun-loving, flamboyant, and vivacious British TV-host wife of Irish rocker Bob Geldof, with whom she had three children. She left Geldof in 1995 to live with Australian rock star Michael Hutchence in a highly publicized and intense love relationship. Paula and Michael were a strong echoist match.

Paula and Michael had one daughter together, Heavenly Hiraani Tiger Lily. She was still a baby when Michael was found hanged in his Sydney hotel bedroom on November 22, 1997. There was much speculation and rumor about his death, which seemed without motive or reason; one theory was that a sex game had gone tragically wrong. On the UK documentary *In Excess: the Death of Michael Hutchence*, shown on August 17, 1999, Paula was adamant that his death must have been an accident.

"He was dangerous and wild," she said. "He could have done anything at any time. But the one thing he wouldn't have done was leave us." Believing that he died from a bizarre sex act was preferable to thinking that she had been deserted.

The pain of grief after Michael's death led Paula further into drugs, and she died as a result of an overdose less than three years after her lover's death. She was found by Tiger Lily (then aged four) on September 17, 2000, dead in bed.

At Michael's funeral, Paula had requested the song "Into your Arms" because it was special to them both as a couple. It was sung by rock star Nick Cave and made her cry on that occasion. Paula's friend Tracy Ayre said that Paula never got over the death of Michael Hutchence. "Into your Arms" was sung again at Paula's funeral. After her death, Tiger Lily, Paula's daughter with Michael, showed her grandfather where she had lived with her mother and told him that mommy and daddy were now happy together in heaven.

*"He was **dangerous** and wild. He could **have done** anything at any time. But the one thing he **wouldn't have done** was leave us."*

Paul and Linda McCartney

In March 1997, when Paul McCartney received his knighthood, he told the assembled press, "It's nice because you get to make your girlfriend a lady—though she always was anyway."

Paul McCartney's grandfather was an Irish coal merchant; Linda's grandfather Eastman (the family name) was a Russian Jewish immigrant to the US. Paul's father was a Liverpool cotton salesman; Linda's won a scholarship to Harvard at the age of 16 and became an eminent lawyer. Paul grew up in public housing in Liverpool, England; Linda spent an affluent childhood in New York surrounded by fabulous art including works by Picasso and de Kooning. Their backgrounds could not have been more different; nor could their love for one another have been greater. The foundation of their love was echoism, which can often bridge the gap between differences in background and

culture. On March 12, 1969, Paul married Linda. Her wedding ring cost £12 ($30) and was bought, he said, just before the store closed. Except for one enforced absence, they did not spend a single night apart during the whole 30 years of their marriage. They were mystified that others may have found this unusual.

The couple had three children together, Mary, Stella, and James (Linda had another daughter, Heather, from a previous marriage). Stella was born by Caesarian section and it was while Paul was waiting outside the operating room (clad in a green surgical gown) that the name of his new

group came to him. The name "Wings" sprang into his mind while he was praying for the safety of his wife and new baby. Linda joined him in the group, becoming from then on wife, mother of his children, professional colleague, and loving companion.

Linda battled with cancer for two years before she died on April 17, 1998, in Arizona. In his official press statement following her death, Paul said, "This is a total heartbreak for my family. Linda was, and still is, the love of my life ... I am privileged to have been her lover for 30 years ... She was unique and the world is a better place for having known her ... her message of love will live on in our hearts forever."

Paul's words were a testament to the deep and unshakable love that he and Linda bore for each other. He was devastated by her death, deprived as he was of the friend and soulmate who had been his companion and lover for 30 years.

Observe the similarities

Linda and Paul's echoist similarities are particularly noticeable around the eyes. Observe the round shape of the eye, the upper eyelid line, and the eyebrows.

Linda's eyes

Paul's eyes

Paul McCartney and Heather Mills

After the death of a mate, it is essential that the surviving partner grieve fully in order to move on to another relationship. Paul did this openly after Linda died in 1998, paying her many public tributes. In July 2001 he became engaged to Heather Mills. Why was he drawn to her after the death of his beloved wife?

*Paul **has reportedly** said that in the **early days** of his relationship with Heather **he cried over Linda** every day—and that it was **Heather** who helped him to come through **the grieving process**.*

The visual attraction between Paul and Linda and Paul and Heather follows a simple equation. The photographs of Paul and Heather (opposite above) show the similarity most particularly in the shapes of their eyes. Their likeness is more pronounced when their faces are viewed from above (opposite below). In these photographs the similarity of their fine-boned noses and the flare of their nostrils becomes more apparent.

Now review the photographs of Paul and Linda on pages 90–91. The visual similarities between them are particularly evident in the region of the eyes. If Paul and Linda had echoism (as they did) and Paul and Heather have echoism (as they do), it is reasonable to suppose that photographs of Linda and Heather will reveal visual similarities between these two ladies.

The photographs below show that this is indeed the case. Heather bears a "look" of Linda, and the proportions of their faces are similar. This is very common among second wives.

Linda's death left a huge hole in Paul's life. He is reported to have said that in the early days of his relationship with Heather he cried over Linda every day, and that it was Heather who helped him to come through the grieving process. His view is that you are lucky to fall so much in love once in a lifetime—and that twice is amazing.

When a successful marriage ends with the death of a partner, the survivor may yearn to repeat the good experience. It is not surprising, therefore, that the second partner often bears a striking resemblance to the first one.

In conclusion

Some people believe that the power of love can be so compelling that a living partner can be "called" by a dead partner to join them and become united in death. Paula Yates never got over the death of her echoist lover Michael Hutchence; her grief and despair perhaps drove her to the abuse of drugs and alcohol that ultimately caused her death. The feeling among her friends is that Paula and Michael are now reunited.

When Linda McCartney died it brought back to Paul a much earlier grief: his mother had died from cancer when he was 14 years old, and he suffered a feeling of terrible emptiness at that time. His mother's memory is preserved in "Let It Be"—the beautiful ballad he wrote based on a dream he had about his mother 10 years after her death. In coming to terms with his loss of Linda, Paul said, "Toward the end of the year that Linda died I wrote a song called 'Magic' about the night I first met her ... I realized that I had turned the corner with that song, because I suddenly thought, I'm really proud to have known someone as beautiful as Linda for 30 years." These words were reported in the British newspaper the *Daily Mail* on November 10, 2001.

Linda and Heather are similar in their behavioral type, both strong and courageous ladies who work for causes close to their hearts. Linda was an ardent campaigner for animal rights and established a world-class vegetarian food company. Heather (now Heather Mills McCartney) had a brilliant modeling career at the time when she was knocked down by a motorcyle in 1993 and lost her left leg below the knee as a result of her injuries. She has maintained her modeling career in spite of this disability, and now campaigns vigorously to rid the world of landmines.

Paul has maintained his attraction to bold, inspiring women. This was the language he learned in his first happy marriage to Linda Eastman, and it is now repeated in his second marriage to Heather Mills.

Why is a **second** partner often similar to the **first**?

John Bayley and **Iris Murdoch**

John Bayley and **Audi Villers**

Individuals who become the second partner often resemble the first either in their behavior pattern or their physical appearance. It would appear that love has its own language. Once learned, that language is not forgotten.

In second marriages or partnerships, people tend to revert to what they know best. In choosing their partners they often repeat their attraction either to the same physical type (including the facial appearance) or to the same behavioral type. The pattern that was established with the first partner is hard to break, and so is repeated—even at the cost of repeating an unhappy situation.

In the folklore of the Jewish tradition dating back thousands of years, the king of Israel is consulted by two widows as to whether they should take new husbands. His advice to the widow who had been unhappily married is to remain alone; the widow who had been happily married is encouraged to marry again.

The die is cast

People who have been contented in marriage are the most likely to want to marry again and relive their happiness. Sometimes behavior patterns established in the old relationship are repeated in the new—perhaps in the choice of a similarly dominant or submissive second partner. It is not just behavior patterns that repeat themselves; often, the second partner will have some of the same physical characteristics as the first.

John Bayley, author and Warton Professor of English at Oxford University from 1974 to 1992, first saw his wife, novelist Iris Murdoch, when she cycled past the window of the dormitory in which he was living. In his memoir *Iris*, written after her death, he told how in that first moment he saw her, he fantasized that "she was simply bicycling about, waiting for me to arrive." Was that the moment he fell in love with her?

John Bayley and Iris Murdoch were an echoist match. The top row of photographs opposite reveals the similarity between them, particularly in the shape of the eyes. The distance between the eye and the brow is the same, and the base of the nose and chin shape are similar. As well as these features, there is a similar expression in the way they hold their mouths.

It is possible that echoist partners who share facial similarities may also have similar character traits. Such partnerships may be better able than others to withstand emotional trauma because the two people share friendship and a special understanding. John enjoyed a long and happy marriage to Iris, and nursed her lovingly at the end after she developed Alzheimer's disease. Since her death, the warm marital behavior pattern that he established with Iris has been repeated with his second wife, Audi Villers, whom he married in June 2000.

A second chance

The echoism John shared with Iris is repeated in his second marriage, to Audi. The second row of photographs opposite reveals the similarity between John and Audi, particularly in the shape of the mouth. There is the same long distance between the nose and the mouth and, like John and Iris, they have similar chins.

Audi and Iris also have echoism. The bottom row of photographs opposite shows the similarities between them in the mouth area and expression, and in the cheeks and chin shape. Audi and her husband Borys had been good friends with the Bayleys for many years. Audi and Iris were close, and close friends may have echoism since like attracts like. If a woman has echoism with her husband and also with one of her close female friends, might her husband also find that friend attractive? If a contented marriage ends with the death of the wife, might the husband be drawn to her echoist friend in an attempt to feel closer to the departed wife or to find happiness again?

"The **three of us** appear to have much **in common,** facially and in terms **of physiognomy**." (Personal letter to the author)

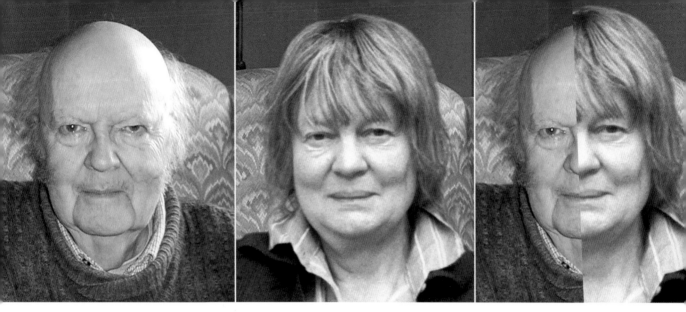

John and Iris have echoism: observe the shape of the eyes, the distance between the eye and the brow, and the base of the nose.

John and Audi have echoism: observe the shape of the mouth, the distance between the nose and the mouth, and the similar chin.

Iris and Audi have echoism: observe the mouth, its expression, and the shape of the cheeks and chin.

In Daphe du Maurier's famous novel *Rebecca*, the narrator marries the domineering Maxim de Winter after the death of his first wife Rebecca. Shy and unglamorous, the anonymous "Mrs. de Winter" struggles with the ghost of the beautiful yet treacherous Rebecca as she tries to supplant her in Maxim's heart and home. Rebecca lives on as a malevolent presence whose shadow creates discord and threatens the marital happiness of the new couple.

The reverse to the situation in *Rebecca* occurs when mutual love for a departed person unites two others; this new syndrome can perhaps be called "acceber" (Rebecca spelled backward). It is easy to apply this to the history of John Bayley, Iris Murdoch, and Audi Villers. John and Iris were an echoist match and enjoyed a happy marriage. Iris, Audi, and John were friends with shared echoist characteristics. As John observed, "the three of us appear to have much in common."

In conclusion

John Bayley repeated physical and behavioral patterns in his second marriage. He is an excellent example of the second marriage syndrome and the wisdom of the king of Israel, namely that those who have been happy in their first marriage should marry a second time.

Paul McCartney and John Bayley were, in their grief, able to draw upon their creative resources, which enabled them to live through and come to terms with the hurt. John Bayley wrote extensively about Iris Murdoch, their life together, their friends, and her illness. Paul paid tribute to Linda through his music. The ability to express their sorrow helped both men to move on to find love and happiness again.

For John and Audi, there was the bonus of a mutual love for Iris. His article in *The Times* of March 19, 2001, following his marriage to Audi, confirmed this. "Neither she nor I had been married in church before, and it seemed to inaugurate a new kind of relationship for us both—our own special kind. Iris seemed to both of us to be at the wedding, in the church she knew so well, and to be smiling down on us." On seeing the likeness between himself, Iris, and Audi in the photographs on page 97, Bayley wrote: "My first wife Iris and my second, Audi, were great friends, and the three of us appear now to have much in common, facially and in terms of physiognomy."

Prima c

opulism

When a man or woman is attracted to their prima copulist love, there is no reason why the object of their love should automatically be attracted to them in return. Prima copulists do not necessarily have any similarity in their facial proportions or shapes.

What is a prima copulist?

A prima copulist is a lover or spouse who resembles a person's first bond, whether that be a mother, nanny, aunt, sister, or father. The prima copulist is often the subject of tempestuous and emotionally charged love that does not count the consequences of embarking upon the relationship.

What is prima copulism?

Prima copulism is an attachment based on a visual resemblance to a person's first bond. The emotional and sexual attachment to the first bond received much publicity in 1920, when Sigmund Freud delivered a series of lectures in Vienna during which he shocked audiences by introducing his theory on infantile sex. His belief was that boys longed for sexual possession of their mothers and that girls fell in love with their fathers and felt hostile to their mothers. In a case where a child is initially looked after by a nanny, Freud maintained that affection, which at first is based on survival, moves in due course from the nanny to the parent. It is possible that the child may remain attached to a first bond who is other than the parent when much time has been spent with this person during the formative years, but in the majority of instances the first love is the mother.

When Freud was making the world aware of the sexual and emotional link between the child and the first bond he did not have the benefit of the equipment we can use in the 21st century to open up research into the visual link. Thanks to photocopiers and computers, it has been possible to carry out research into the visual process of the theory that Freud described—in other words, that we fall in love visually at an early age and subconsciously carry that image in our head throughout our lives.

Moreover, when in adulthood we meet the person who resembles the first bond, our natural instinct is to fall in love as we did all those years ago in the cradle.

Prima copulism is a primal love, often fired with some of the needs and insecurities of childhood. If a person's first bond is subsequently absent during the early years, the greater the need for the feeling of completion that only the first bond can give. Often men jump into such a relationship without caution, regardless of their responsibilities or position. Instinctively they trust the woman because this is the love that goes back to the cradle, where trust and affection were first learned. If one trusts a partner, many obstacles are instinctively surmounted. Generally, a woman in a prima copulist relationship has great power. After all, mother (or nanny) always knows best.

Prima copulist love burns with great intensity, and it is possible to reach the highest highs emotionally. Although the mother figure is trusted, this is a possessive love where affection cannot be shared. It is passionate, often beset with jealousy (note the jealousy of the young child for his or her first bond). There is nothing cool or controlled about prima copulism. It is involuntary and usually overwhelming, leaving the protagonist open and vulnerable. The success of these intense love affairs often depends on how one's ability to give and receive love has been affected by early childhood experiences. Peaceful coexistence may be difficult, but being apart from the object of desire hurts even more. People who divorce and remarry the same person several times are often prima copulists.

*Prima copulist love **burns** with great **intensity**. With such a love it is possible to reach the highest highs **emotionally**.*

THE VISUAL DEFINITION OF PRIMA COPULISM

The prima copulist will resemble the protagonist's first bond at the time the bond was created. For example, if a man's mother was a slim, auburn-haired woman when she was rocking him in the cradle, then the prima copulist love object will resemble his mother at that time rather than the woman she aged into in later years. This is important, because that image is held in his subconscious mind's eye from the cradle for many years until he might perceive her resemblance in another woman in adulthood. If there are two sons with a great age difference and the mother has significantly changed in appearance between the birth of both children, the younger son's prima copulist ideal and that of his older brother will be different.

The man is usually unaware of the woman's resemblance to his first bond because his attraction operates on a subconscious level. The aging process affecting the prima copulist does not alter the man's love for her, in the same way that wrinkles and sagging flesh never altered his affection for his mother or other first bond. His love is stronger than that. In fact, if a prima copulist woman is aware of her role in the relationship she may be best advised not to undergo cosmetic surgery, since some of her likeness to her man's first love may be lost during the process.

The prima copulist woman may often look more like the man's mother than her own. When looking at wedding photographs, it is interesting to note the mother of the groom. Frequently she will resemble her new daughter-in-law, either in her smile, her general head shape, or the shape of her features. The strongest love is that of the young child for his mother, and a prima copulist adult relationship is fueled by a longing to get back to the safety of that love.

Could the **Mona Lisa** be an early visual example **of** prima copulist **love**?

Mona Lisa and **Leonardo da Vinci**

The Mona Lisa is the most famous painting in the world, and there are many theories as to who the woman with the enigmatic expression and gentle smile might be. Some believe that the model was actually a man, and may even have been a self-portrait of Leonardo himself, since there is a discernible likeness between artist and sitter.

According to Giorgio Vasari, who wrote the book *Lives of the Most Eminent Italian Architects, Painters, and Sculptors*, first published in 1550 and still in print today, the model was a young Florentine woman named Lisa Gherardini. She was the wife of a wealthy man named Francesco del Giocondo—hence, the popular name of La Gioconda by which the painting is often known.

A labor of love?

The *Mona Lisa* was begun in 1503 and took an extraordinary four years to complete. Leonardo even employed musicians to entertain his subject during the sittings so that she did not weary of the process.

This is the only existing portrait done by the artist in his hand alone, and it seems to have been a labor of love, since it was not commissioned by her husband or, it is thought, by anyone else. Upon its completion Leonardo was unusually reluctant to part with it, taking it with him to Milan and then to France. It was eventually acquired by King François I, either directly from Leonardo himself or from his heirs following his death.

In the *Mona Lisa* and the only known self-portrait of Leonardo in 1512 (here reversed), it can be seen that the artist and his sitter are harmonists, sharing the same facial proportions. Observe the distances between the main features and their tall, round foreheads. There is also a degree of echoism, seen in the similar shape of their eyes.

Not only did Leonardo and La Gioconda have harmonism and echoism, but it would also appear that they share a similarity with his mother, who was his first bond. Leonardo was born on April 15, 1452, in the small town of Vinci, near Florence, the illegitimate son of a notary, Ser Piero da Vinci, and one of his family's servants, a peasant woman named Caterina. It is thought that within the year Caterina was despatched

from the household, leaving her infant son to be brought up by his father and the wife he had just married, Albiera di Giovanni Amadori.

Although Leonardo "lost" his mother at this early age, surviving letters show that he was in contact with her during her later years. In her old age she went to live with him in Milan, and there is evidence that he paid for her burial. The woman in the reversed sketch (opposite below) is widely believed to have been his mother. The likeness between her and Leonardo (opposite above) is self-evident, and she also resembles the Mona Lisa, shown left in the picture above.

Sigmund Freud believed that the mysterious smile of the Mona Lisa aroused in Leonardo a repressed memory of his mother's smile, lost to him when he was an infant. According to Freud, his fascination with it was so great that he tried subsequently to reproduce this blissful smile in all his paintings of women.

*Freud believed that the **smile of the Mona Lisa** aroused in Leonardo a **repressed memory** of his mother's smile.*

In conclusion

It is possible that Leonardo felt the joy of discovering prima copulist love for La Gioconda. This might also account for the fact that in Leonardo's subsequent paintings of the Madonna her face frequently bore some resemblance to that of La Gioconda.

The secret of the painting's genius may be the fact that the artist himself felt bathed in golden light—a warmth derived from being reunited with the eternal mother for whom he craved, in the persona of La Gioconda. The specialness of their relationship may explain the mystery behind the enigmatic smile, both alluring and self-assured; perhaps her confidence came from a knowledge of the effect she had upon her portraitist. How the painting came into the possession of François I will probably never be known for certain, but some diarists say that Leonardo even gave instructions for the painting to be buried with him. No matter how the artist was finally parted from his masterpiece, five hundred years later we can look upon the object of prima copulist love in the *Mona Lisa* and share the wonderment felt by Leonardo as he beheld her.

What **kind** of love **lies behind** **modern-day** fairy tales**?**

Crown Prince Willem Alexander and **Maxima Zorreguieta**

We all know the fairy tales in which a girl from an unlikely background marries a handsome prince—but similar tales certainly do happen in real life. These occur most usually within the prima copulist category, elevating commoners to royalty and propelling ordinary folk into the heady realms of a jetset lifestyle in the blink of an eye.

At a fiesta in Seville, Spain, Crown Prince Willem Alexander of the Netherlands met Maxima Zorreguieta, an Argentinian on vacation from her job as a banker in New York City.

Maxima reportedly did not know for some time that Willem had royal connections. Hence began a romance between the heir to the royal house of Orange-Nassau and the young girl whose background should without question have excluded her as a potential bride and the future queen of the Netherlands. Maxima Zorreguieta is the daughter of Jorge Zorreguieta, who was the agriculture minister during the brutal military dictatorship of Jorge Videla in Argentina. Under Videla's regime, 30,000 people vanished. They are known as the Disappeared.

Love conquers all

The match between Willem and Maxima was tested by the greatest critics: fierce public controversy and political opposition. There were fears of a constitutional crisis and demands for Willem to choose between his love and the throne. In addition to the background of Maxima's father, the couple embraced different religions. Maxima is Roman Catholic and wished to retain her faith, while Willem is the future monarch of a Protestant country.

However, none of these obstacles deterred Willem. There was never any question of his forsaking Maxima Zorreguieta, because she is his prima copulist love; she has the same "look" as his mother. The similarity between Maxima and Queen Beatrix of the Netherlands is apparent around the soft rounded base of the nose and the slightly prominent upper set of the teeth. The shape of the face and chin also bear similarity.

Since Maxima and Queen Beatrix also have similar expressions, there is a likelihood that the two women will age in a similar fashion. Young or old, svelte or otherwise, a prima copulist is always held in the same regard by her man. In fact, the aging process for a prima copulist love should be less alarming than for many other women because frequently time continues to shape her likeness toward that of the older, much-cherished first bond.

In February 2002 Crown Prince Willem married Maxima, who won over the people of the Netherlands and is now called the "Dutch Diana." In the church where they married there were 30,000 flowers—"almost one for each of the Disappeared," said one protestor from the University of Groningen. At the wedding every dynasty of Europe was represented and no fewer than 70 members of Europe's royal families gathered to watch the union of the blissfully happy couple whose love nearly split a nation.

*There was never **any question** of Willem forsaking Maxima Zorreguieta, because she is his **prima copulist** love.*

In conclusion

The strongest love is that of the child with his first bond. When, as an adult, he meets a person who represents his internal picture of that first bond, he feels an immediate kinship and a feeling of completeness.

It was to Queen Beatrix's credit that she became the staunchest supporter of her son's choice of bride. Opposition would not have derailed this union, no matter which quarter it came from. Those who belong to the prima copulist love category are not swayed by reason, or by consideration of money, family, religion, or background. Love conquers all.

Why can **no** woman rival Camilla Parker Bowles for **Charles's** heart?

Prince Charles and Camilla Parker Bowles

Prince Charles was in the grounds of Windsor Great Park on a windy, rainy day when he first met Camilla Shand. Charles was 22 years old, fresh from Cambridge University. Camilla was 23. They chatted animatedly for more than an hour, and so commenced a relationship that has to date spanned more than 30 years.

Many are mystified by the love that has bound Charles to Camilla for so long, unable to understand why Charles would favor her over his former wife, Princess Diana—in her time widely considered to be one of the most glamorous women in the world. How could Camilla, good-natured, constant, and down to earth, triumph over the challenge presented by a beautiful princess? From a visual perspective, the answer is simple: Camilla is Prince Charles's prima copulist love.

A face from the past

It is said that love is blind, but in fact love sees very well. It takes in the look of a person in the blink of an eye, so much faster than the speed of thought that there is no time to realize the subconscious workings of attraction. Love at first sight does not have time to take account of a woman's nature. It is purely visual.

The story behind the long romance between Charles and Camilla begins in the late 1940s when Mabel Anderson, daughter of an Essex policeman, was given sole charge of the new-born prince. Friends and courtiers tended to see Mabel as a surrogate mother, and she was the first person to whom Charles invariably turned for support, comfort, and advice. As a rule, Prince Charles saw his mother, the queen, just two times a day, for half an hour at 9:00 a.m. and again at 4:30 p.m. They were loving interludes, but sadly the weight of office did not permit her to spend the time she would have liked with her first-born. The queen was, and still is, the most traveled sovereign in history, devoting herself to her country and the countries of the Commonwealth with a tireless and often painful self-discipline.

Charles's first birthday was spent alone with Mabel Anderson, since the queen had accompanied the Duke of Edinburgh on his tour of naval duty in Malta. Shown left is a photograph of Charles on his second birthday, being wheeled in the park by Mabel, his "Mispy"—that is the nickname he gave to her. His mother was absent yet again, on a royal tour of Canada, on his third birthday. The queen has always placed her royal duties above all other considerations at great personal cost, and one wonders how often, at formal state occasions, she was wishing she could be like other mothers, tucking her children into bed and reading them a story. Reportedly, the queen missed Charles's first step, his first tooth, and his first word, which was "Nana." His beloved nanny Mispy filled the role of mother instead.

In *The Prince of Wales*, the biography of Charles's life written by Jonathan Dimbleby, Charles describes Mabel as "warm," "loving," "sympathetic," "gentle," and "caring." These adjectives, which are often employed to describe a mother, are also the qualities Charles has ascribed to Camilla Parker Bowles.

*In **Camilla Parker Bowles** Charles has found the **woman** who resembles his **beloved nanny Mispy**—Mabel Anderson.*

Mabel Anderson and Camilla Parker Bowles may be from different backgrounds but they are cast in the same mold. Camilla looks remarkably like Charles's nanny did when he first knew her in infancy—the crucial time for the prima copulist bond to be established. They share the same-shaped head and face: subconsciously this is what the opposite sex first notices. That is why people are drawn to those who often have the same "look." Seen from a three-quarter angle, the likeness between the two is even stronger.

Were it not for Charles's position as heir to the throne, no doubt he would have married Camilla in the early seventies. However, the rules that governed his choice of bride were strict: she had to be a Protestant, which eliminated a number of European princesses who would have been accustomed to a life of royal protocol; and while a bride drawn from the ranks of the British aristocracy would be an alternative, she would have to be someone pure and pliant. Camilla was not suitable as far as the royal establishment was concerned—but in the end prima copulism proved stronger than duty.

The bond between Prince Charles and Mabel Anderson has grown no less intense throughout his life, and he entrusted her with the care of his own sons, William and Harry, when they spent time with him while he was separated from Princess Diana. In Camilla Parker Bowles Charles has found a woman who resembles his beloved nanny Mabel Anderson—not only physically, but also as the same emotional rock, comforter, and symbol of warrmth.

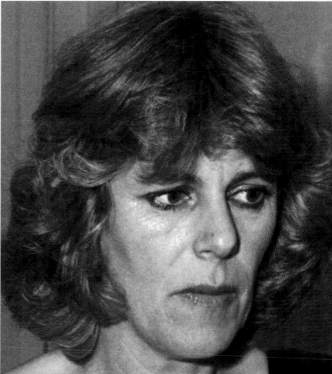

Observe the similarities

Character is read in the eyes and nature is read in the mouth. Since the eyes and mouth of Camilla and Mabel are so similar it is no wonder that Charles used the same adjectives to describe them both. Look-alikes invariably are alike.

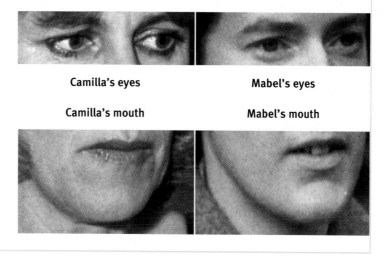

Camilla's eyes **Mabel's eyes**

Camilla's mouth **Mabel's mouth**

Observe the similarities

- short distance between eye and upper lid
- mouth which, when smiling, turns downwards
- set of the upper teeth
- same-shaped chin and jawline

Their faces are not only in the same proportion, but also have the same shape in the central features—eyes and mouth. Half of Camilla's face may be easily substituted on Mabel's face. It is as though they are pieces in an interchangeable jigsaw.

Finding support

It is not just that Camilla looks like Mabel that is relevant. Since Charles uses the same adjectives to describe both women he most probably responds to them similarly, with unguarded affection and trust.

More pertinently, Camilla responds to Charles with a familiar behavioral pattern, the same that he had established with his first bond, Mabel. Such familiarity, grounded in his infancy, no doubt brings enormous relaxation and offers welcome relief from the pressures of duty, protocol, and a critical press.

*Camilla was not suitable as far as the **royal establishment** was concerned—but **prima copulism** proved stronger than duty.*

In conclusion

The lives of those excluded from easy social interaction, whether by celebrity, wealth, high office, or notoriety, can be isolated. Nowhere is this more true than in the case of British royalty, with its formality and duty. The summit of any social mountain might be attractive but it can also be a cold and lonely place. Consequently, people in this position tend to be most vulnerable to the appeal of warm, loving relationships; and unfortunately, because of their status, pay a heavy price in terms of the world's scrutiny if they stray outside their marriages.

In Charles's world, many are strained and unrelaxed with him because of his royal position. A normal interaction would be valued greatly, spelling warmth, relaxation, and security—in a word, home. A warm behavioral pattern understood from childhood is the familiar language which a person would wish to recapture throughout his adult life. At the end of the day, doesn't everyone just want to come home?

It may be noted that over the past 31 years, no matter how great the intrusions into her private life, Camilla has remained loyal, dignified, and remarkably strong. Many people would not have been able to withstand the unpleasant pressures to which she has been regularly subjected.

Is **caution** thrown to the **wind** when **a man** meets his prima copulist love**?**

John F. Kennedy Jr. and **Carolyn Bessette**

If a child has a highly disciplined upbringing, will this affect his control when he meets his prima copulist love? Will his childhood restrain his passion or modify his behavior?

It seems not—for the child who famously saluted the coffin of his father, President John F. Kennedy, with such self-restraint grew into the man who wept uncontrollably on the curbside after a quarrel with his girlfriend.

John F. Kennedy Jr. was the son of Jackie, the first lady. Her absences, accompanying JFK on presidential business, would have created a strong need in the boy for a maternal figure. Once John found his prima copulist love with Carolyn Bessette, who had the "look" of Jackie, the thought of losing her was intolerable.

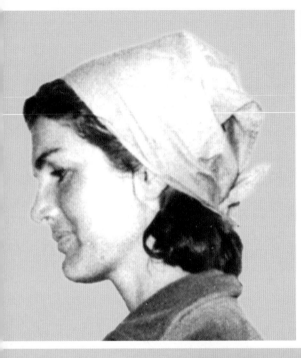
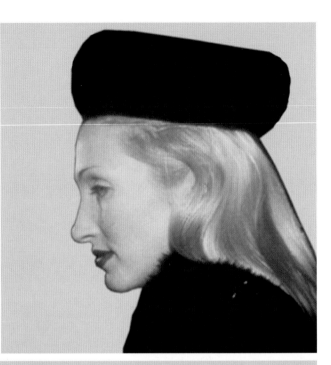

*In the blink of an eye, Carolyn Bessette became the **prima copulist** love of the most **eligible bachelor** in the world.*

Instant attraction

When John F. Kennedy Jr. first saw Carolyn Bessette, reportedly when she was rollerblading in New York City's Central Park, was it love at first sight?

Prima copulist love takes in the "look" of a person in a second, even if a resemblance to the first bond is momentary and fleeting. Perhaps

John F. Kennedy Jr. subconsciously recognized Carolyn's profile as having a resemblance to his mother's. In the blink of an eye, the supremely stylish Carolyn Bessette (at that time a mid-level publicist for Calvin Klein) became the prima copulist love of the most eligible bachelor in the world. John F. Kennedy Jr. once told a friend, "I'm attracted to strong-willed women like my mother." (Edward Klein, *The Kennedy Curse*)

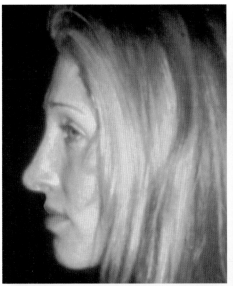

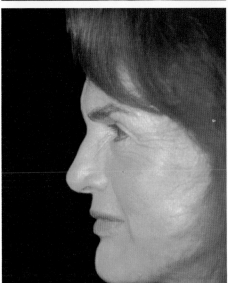

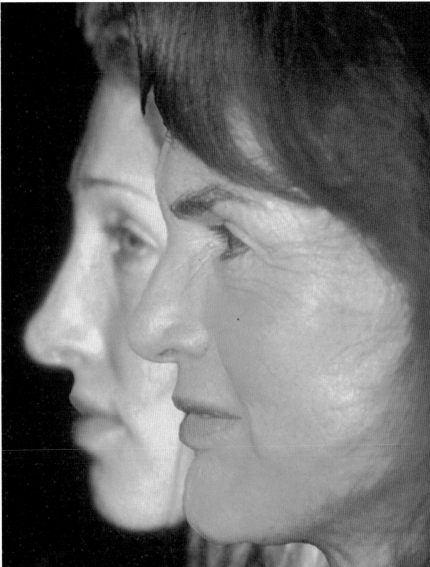

In conclusion

When John F. Kennedy Jr. was 13 years old he was mugged in Central Park. According to FBI files, his mother, Jackie, considered it a useful experience, an attitude that some might find cold. After John Jr. married Carolyn Bessette, she was dubbed "the ice queen." Coolness and detachment was a language that John Jr. understood.

Was this already Carolyn's behavior when he met her, making her attractive to John because of his own mothering? Or could it be that he subconsciously fashioned her to reflect the behavioral pattern with which he was familiar? In other words, do men who love in a prima copulist manner require their women to resemble their first bond not only in looks but also in behavior?

A disciplined upbringing of rigorous self-control does not affect the highly emotional response to prima copulist love. Stormy marriage-counseling sessions, jealous tantrums, and ferocious arguments recorded on prime-time television were all part of the pain John and Carolyn inflicted upon one another. This was prima copulist love in which the participants were driven to the heights and depths in a merry-go-round of passion.

Does **prima copulist** love ever really **die**, even when a couple are **separated**?

Richard Burton and Elizabeth Taylor

"She was, I decided, the most astonishingly self-contained, pulchritudinous, remote, removed, inaccessible woman I had ever seen. She was unquestionably gorgeous. I can think of no other way to describe a combination of plenitude, frugality, abundance, tightness. She was lavish. She was a dark unyielding largesse. She was, in short, too bloody much and not only that, she was totally ignoring me."

Richard Burton's description on first seeing Elizabeth Taylor, quoted in David Jenkins's book *Richard Burton: a Brother Remembered*, sums up the devastating attraction that she exerted over him from the moment they met on a film set in 1963.

Richard was the son of Edith Thomas, a barmaid who married miner Dic Jenkins in 1900 and bore no fewer than 13 children in 26 years. Two years after Richard was born his mother died and he was then brought up by his much older sister Cecilia James, who cherished him and whom he adored.

A search for a sister

**In Richard Burton's book *A Christmas Story*, which
was published in 1965—two years after he met
Elizabeth Taylor—he wrote, "My sister was no
ordinary woman—no woman ever is, but to me,
my sister less than any. When my mother died
she, my sister, had become my mother and more
mother to me than any mother could have been.**

I was immensely proud of her. I shone in the
reflection of her green-eyed, black-haired, gypsy
beauty . . . It wasn't until 30 years later when
I saw her in another woman, Elizabeth Taylor,
that I realized I had been searching for her
all my life."

Richard Burton's sister Cecilia James (shown
above) shares much facial similarity with

Elizabeth Taylor. The two women both have the same large, soulful eyes and a similarly gentle smile.

Elizabeth Taylor has had eight marriages to seven husbands. She and Richard are probably the most famous couple to have tied the knot for a second time. They met and fell in love on the set of the film *Cleopatra*, and the intensity of their tempestuous romance aroused fascinated interest from the press and public worldwide. They were married in 1964, but after a decade of diamonds, spats, kissing and making up the couple divorced in June 1974. Sixteen months later they married again, but by August 1, 1976, it was all over, this time for good. Elizabeth Taylor said of their relationship that they loved each other too much.

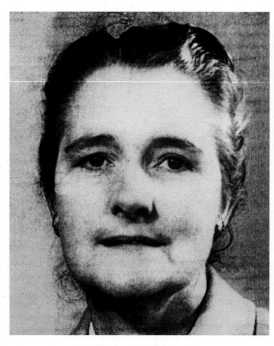 

Many said that their love was so strong that they found it impossible to live together and impossible to live apart. Certainly their arguments were legendary.

Burton loved Elizabeth as a young woman and with equal intensity as she matured. It can be seen from the photographs on these pages how much the mature Elizabeth resembles Burton's sister Cecilia James in her later years.

Elizabeth Taylor went with Richard Burton to Buckingham Palace when he received his O.B.E (Order of the British Empire). On May 16, 2000, 16 years after Burton's death on August 5, 1984, Elizabeth went to Buckingham Palace again, this time on her own, to become a Dame Commander of the Order of the British Empire. On her wedding finger she wore the fabulous 33.19 carat Krupp diamond that Burton had given her. He had bought it for her in 1968 when she became the first actress to earn a million dollars for a film. It was the memory of Richard Burton that brought her close to tears in the forecourt of Buckingham Palace on that day in May 2000. She told the assembled press, "I miss him so much. I wish he were here."

Although the relationship was declared over on August 1, 1976, some say that if Richard Burton had not died, he and Elizabeth Taylor might have come together for a third time. Prima copulism, which is an exhausting, passionate love, may not always be "over"—even when it's over.

*Some say that if Richard Burton had **not died,** he and Elizabeth Taylor might have **come together** for a third time.*

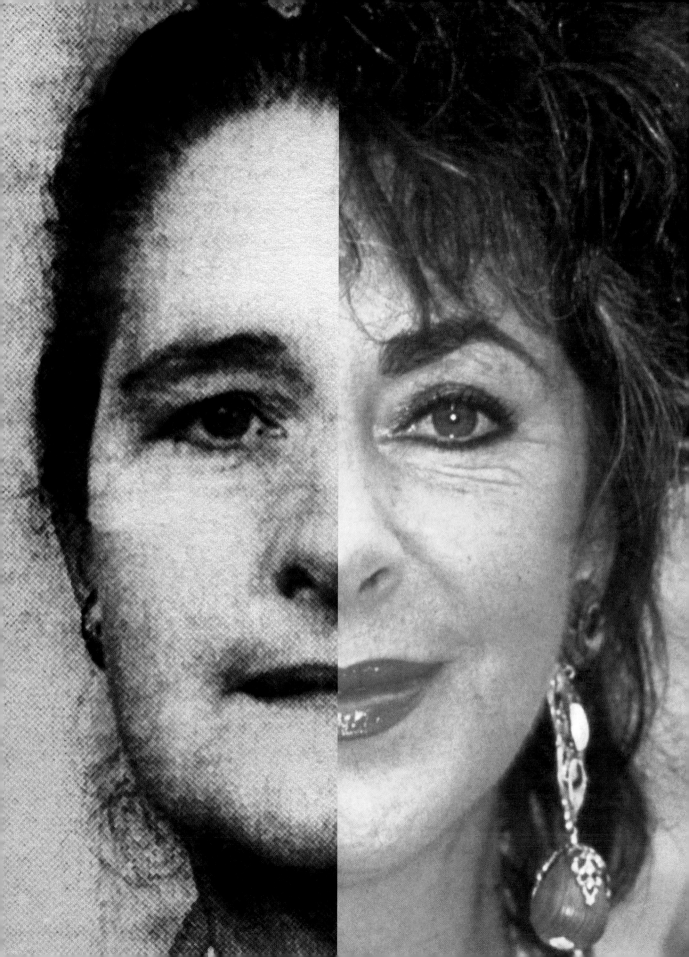

In conclusion

Burton was much loved by his sister and therefore he was able to receive and give love in later life. Nonetheless, the trauma of separation from a mother still does damage. The subconscious longing for a mother often results in a creative sublimation. In Richard Burton's case he sublimated his longing into acting.

When a person falls in prima copulist love he or she is reuniting with the first bond. If one has known separation from a loved one as a child, the feeling of insecurity tends to fuel emotional need—hence, the reunited love is very strong. It is passionate love often driven by possessiveness and by fear of losing the love object once again. The intensity with which Richard Burton loved Elizabeth Taylor captured the imagination of the whole world. People flocked to see their films and glimpse the magic of their love.

Why was **Napoleon** so crazy for **Josephine**, an older woman with a **dubious past?**

Napoleon and Josephine

Napoleon said of Josephine that he truly loved her, but did not respect her. He thought her a liar and an utter spendthrift, but she had a certain something that he found irresistible. To him, she was a woman to her very fingertips.

Corsican-born Napoleon Bonaparte was a military genius and tactician who eventually rose to be the emperor of France. In 1795, he met Martinique-born Rose de Beauharnais, otherwise known as Josephine. A widow with two children and a succession of lovers, she dazzled the relatively innocent Napoleon.

A famous match

Already successful, Napoleon could have had the pick of France for a wife, despite his overly large head and diminutive height. He chose Josephine.

Historians and psychologists alike have pondered the question of why Napoleon, still in his twenties, married the 33-year-old Josephine, whose beauty was on the wane and who had bad teeth, which were described as "brown as cloves." Josephine was extravagant, feather-

brained, faithless, cunning, and ruthless, with a sex drive that stopped just short of nymphomania. A former lover had rejected her on the grounds that one may take a prostitute for a mistress but not for a wife. However, the pictures of Napoleon and Josephine above and on the facing page provide some of the answers; they have echoism, with the same expression and curvaceous top lip, and remarkably similar eyes.

Josephine had lost her first husband, Alexandre de Beauharnais, to the guillotine during the

French Revolution and was lucky to escape it herself. Saved by the overthrow of Robespierre shortly before her own execution, she became mistress to men who were able to provide for her and her two children. Napoleon, then a major general in the French army, had ambition and promise. Fifteen days after their first meeting in 1795 he fell into her trap, and they became lovers.

After he first made love to Josephine, Napoleon wrote her an impassioned letter referring to the intoxicating evening they had spent together. Six months later they were married. On the eve of the wedding Josephine slept with General Barras, her former lover, who as a wedding present gave Napoleon supreme command of Italy. He was thus quickly dispatched abroad, and Josephine was left free to resume her affair with Barras, one of many that continued throughout her marriage. At one point, six days after writing a tender letter describing how much he yearned to be present at her evening undressing, Napoleon arrived for a rendezvous with his wife to find that she had left for the arms of yet another lover.

A mother's love?

Napoleon was so heartbroken at finding her gone that he almost fainted from shock. Later that day he seems to have had a fit of some kind before writing her a letter in which he described the incurable pain she had caused him.

Napoleon was often publicly humiliated by Josephine's unrestrained behavior, in particular when a letter to her from her son, containing information that Napoleon knew of a certain affair, was intercepted and published in the London *Morning Chronicle* and, later, in the French press.

At one point, he barred Josephine from their house and sent her huge wardrobe of clothes to the porter's lodge with instructions that he must not admit her. Josephine was able to soften the porter's heart with her tears and persuaded her children to plead with Napoleon until he relented and let her in. Angry reproaches were followed by heated sexual encounters. Apparently the next day they were found contentedly in bed. This love behavior is typically prima copulist in its intensity. But from that day onward, Josephine lost the upper hand she had maintained in their relationship and instead Napoleon gained the psychological advantage.

Napoleon also had many affairs, the most famous of which was with Marie Waleska, a Polish countess whom he met when his forces occupied Warsaw in 1807. However, Napoleon never stopped loving Josephine, for she was his prima copulist love; she resembled Napoleon's mother Letizia (see facing page, below and right). Their chins, eyebrows, top lips, and upper eyelids are similar in shape.

The important early parental influence in Napoleon's life came from his mother. There was often a clash of strong wills between mother and son, when Letizia was wont to use a whip on him. She was a stern taskmaster who punished her son for the slightest misdemeanor. On one occasion when he was eight years old she threatened him with a beating for behaving badly in church, where he was an altar boy. She apparently relented in response to his pleas for mercy but later that day, when he had taken off his clothes, she set about him with a whip. It was just one of many occasions when she betrayed Napoleon's trust. In adulthood, his greatest love was reserved for a similarly untrustworthy woman.

Although in many respects Josephine and Letizia were completely different in character, in their relationship to Napoleon they were similar. His comment that he really did love Josephine but had no respect for her mirrored his feelings for his mother, whom he did not respect because of suspicions of her infidelity with Marbeuf, the military governor of Corsica. For her part, Letizia hated Josephine and, like Napoleon's siblings, urged him to divorce her. When Countess Marie Waleska became pregnant Napoleon knew for sure that he was capable of

*Napoleon's comment that he **really did love** Josephine but had no respect for her mirrored his relationship with **his mother**.*

fathering an heir to the throne of France and thus the days of his childless marriage with Josephine were finally numbered.

For some time Napoleon resisted the pressure to divorce Josephine that was exerted on him by family and courtiers alike, protesting that she had brought delight to his private life and he would be showing ingratitude for all she had done for him. One night, when Napoleon was taken ill with stomach cramps, Josephine abandoned a visit to a ball and came to his bedside in her finery. Napoleon pulled her toward him, crying that he couldn't possibly leave her. They made love and spent the night together, setting aside the question of divorce.

In 1810, when Napoleon finally confirmed his resolve to divorce her, screams were heard from the Imperial Salon where Josephine lay prostrate on the carpet shrieking until she was carried to her rooms. At the formal public announcement of their divorce, Napoleon, the tough military man, sat down in tears after he had thanked Josephine for 13 memorable years. That same night Josephine broke into Napoleon's apartments and kissed him passionately. The next day she departed for Malmaison, the country chateau a few miles from Paris that would henceforth be her home. Napoleon accompanied her and they walked hand in hand in the rain through the gardens. He was careful not to embrace her or to enter the chateau, for he could not quite trust himself to resist his prima copulist love.

As for Josephine, in a letter to Napoleon after the divorce she expressed gratitude that he had not forgotten her, saying that her thanks were as tender as the love she would always bear him.

In conclusion

In many ways Napoleon's relationship with Josephine mirrored that with his mother: lack of trust, betrayal, and disappointment were combined with love. Both women were capable of cruelty toward him. Freud felt sure that Napoleon's attraction to Josephine was influenced by his own love and need for the mother figure, especially since Josephine was six years his senior.

Although Freud made the emotional connection between Letizia and Josephine, he made no mention of the visual similarity between the two. The prima copulism of Napoleon and Josephine is a key example of how a strong facial resemblance between mother and daughter-in-law evokes powerful love in a man. No doubt many cases of the people analyzed by Freud as having some sort of mother complex could also be fruitfully examined with regard to their partner's physical similarity to their first bond.

Can **the void** ever be filled when **prima copulist** love is thwarted**?**

Princess Margaret and **Peter Townsend**

Madonna and **Sean Penn**

In this section several examples of prima copulist love between a man and a mother figure have been examined. Women too can fall in love with someone who resembles their first bond—but in this case it will be their childhood father figure.

Biologically, men are the "hunters," and it is they who win over their mates. Can a man, when he is the object of prima copulist love, be won over when he is not attracted by a woman's looks? It is unlikely, since a man does not usually fall in love with a woman he finds unattractive.

Is prima copulist love for a male figure characterized by the same intensity as that for a female? Does the closeness of a female to her first male bond during early childhood create a similarly strong need in the adult woman when she meets her prima copulist match in later life?

Princess Margaret and Peter Townsend

Princess Margaret, whose relationship with Peter Townsend may have influenced the rest of her life, is one example of a woman who found a prima copulist love.

The Princess, adored daughter of King George VI and sister of the present queen, first met Group Captain Townsend in a corridor in Buckingham Palace when she was 14. He was a married man of 30, with the position of equerry to the king. In 1952, following the king's death, Townsend went to work for both the queen mother and the princess, who was now 22. By now Townsend's marriage was in its last painful stages and by the end of 1952 he had been granted a divorce from his wife, Rosemary. A secret and intense courtship then took place between Princess Margaret and Townsend. In the spring of 1953,

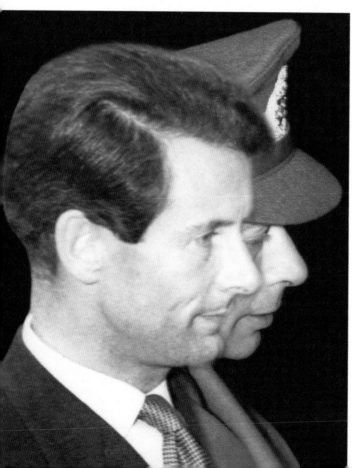

at Windsor Castle, Townsend told the princess that he loved her, and she replied that she felt the same for him.

Princess Margaret was instantly attracted to Townsend. The visual similarity between him and George VI, which lies chiefly in their profiles, is quite marked. They both had a lean head shape, were fine-boned and sensitive-looking, and had aquiline noses, with similarly shaped nostrils. An unusual characteristic was the area between the nostril and upper lip, where the slant toward the mouth was similar. The lips were fine-drawn and thin, and both had firm but not over-strong chins. Perhaps Princess Margaret related to them with a similar dynamic, whereby she could depend on them without feeling dominated.

It was less than 20 years since Edward VIII had abdicated the throne to marry a divorcée, Wallis Simpson. To the royal family and to the Church, marriage between the princess and a divorced man was equally unacceptable. Townsend was transferred to Belgium for two years in an attempt to end the relationship, but the enforced parting only increased the intensity of their love. However, in October 1955, following two months of intense pressure from the royal family, the Establishment, and the Church, Margaret was forced to reach a decision over her future. She released a statement which read: "Mindful of the Church's teaching that Christian marriage is indissoluble, and conscious of my duty to the Commonwealth, I have decided to put these considerations before any others."

The queen mother, unable to contain her sadness for her daughter, reportedly cried openly when discussing Townsend and Margaret with the royal household. Margaret, for her part, never forgave Sir Alan Lascelles, the courtier who was responsible for Townsend's exile to Belgium. Years later she referred to Lascelles as the man who had ruined her life.

Although the relationship was officially over, Townsend and Margaret saw each other intermittently for three more years. Townsend returned to Brussels from where, in 1959, he wrote to the Princess to tell her that he was marrying a Belgian, Marie Luce Ramagne. She bore a strong resemblance to Margaret.

Princess Margaret married society photographer Anthony Armstrong-Jones in May 1960 and had two children by him. Ironically, in 1978 she became the first royal to obtain a divorce. Although she formed subsequent relationships, none brought her lasting happiness. She died in 2002 and, breaking with royal tradition, was cremated so that her ashes could be laid to rest alongside those of her much-loved "Papa," George VI.

*In the spring of 1953, at **Windsor Castle,** Townsend told the princess that he **loved** her. She replied that she felt the same.*

Madonna and Sean Penn

The facial similarities between actor Sean Penn and Madonna's father, Silvio Ciccone, are umistakable. Note the shapes of their noses, the shape and expression of their eyes, and the sturdy set of their chins.

It is not difficult, therefore, to see Madonna's prima copulist attraction to her first husband, Sean Penn. By all accounts this relationship was typical of prima copulist behavior in its tempestuous and often volatile nature. The couple were married in 1985 in a blaze of publicity but, after they had been together for just two years, the relationship ended in 1987.

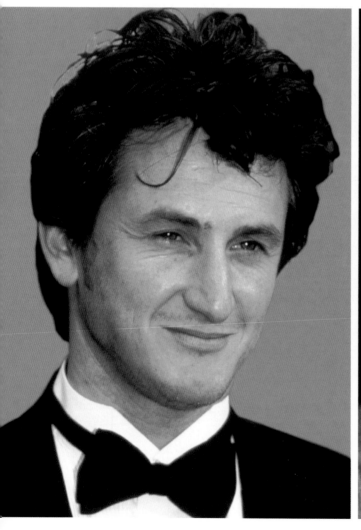

In conclusion

Through the examples given in this section, Sigmund Freud's theory on infantile sex can for the first time be supported with visual evidence. The relationship that the male child forms with the mother figure is in later life the basis for a strong love for someone who has the same "look." Although female examples of Freud's theory do not offer themselves so readily, women can also fall in love with a man who resembles their first male bond. Freud made the emotional link, but apparently did not make the visual link that is shown here.

The prima copulist is loved with a focus and energy that excludes all others. In the case of Prince Charles, most people would have imagined that Diana's youth, beauty, and charming naivety would have given her a distinct advantage over Camilla Parker Bowles, older, less glamorous, and apparently more suitable as a comfortable friend than a love match. However, Camilla is Prince Charles's prima copulist love and as such has held his affections for decades. If someone is loved in a prima copulist way, that love is beyond consideration of their age, beauty, wealth, or position. Generally one can never replace this category of love with a passion of equal intensity. It is only for the very fortunate that prima copulist love is mutual, with both partners recognizing their first bond in each other. More usually, while one partner will be attracted by prima copulism, the other will need a degree of echoism or harmonism to sustain the relationship and return affection.

If a loved person represents an internal picture of the first bond, no one else can compare with the unique attachment that is formed and the feeling of completion that it brings. Group Captain Townsend, who resembled King George VI, stepped into the affections of Princess Margaret after the death of her beloved father. Her grief sent her into a spiral of depression and loneliness which was understood by Townsend, who knew how she felt having witnessed the father-daughter bond from close quarters. Townsend was the prima copulist love of Princess Margaret. Although she was never reunited with him, when her ashes were laid beside the remains of George VI 50 years to the day after the king's funeral, she was in death reunited with her beloved Papa.

Having

it all

When a couple have all three of the visual love categories in their relationship, they have it all. The love of a person resembling the first bond (the most powerful visual love category) is combined with the shared characteristics of harmonism and echoism.

Elton John and David Furnish

Elton John met Toronto-born filmmaker David Furnish at a mutual friend's dinner party in 1994. Elton was instantly attracted to David and by the end of the evening they had exchanged telephone numbers. The following day David went to visit Elton, they shared a Chinese carry-out meal—and they have been together ever since. Elton has discussed the possibility of marriage to David, whom he describes as his soulmate.

The photograph on the facing page demonstrates the echoism shared by the pair. Their most striking similarity is the shape of their mouths, which is unusual. The top lip seems to be fastened in the centre and bows out on either side in an identical way (see also p. 148).

In a rare joint interview with Britain's *Sunday Times Culture* magazine (December 2, 2001),

Elton said, "It is essential for me to be with someone as creatively inspired as me, and David is. We have long conversations about movies, books, films, records, art, photography." While Elton and David may both have had many of these interests before they met, the nature of echoism is that each takes on the interests of the other. The couple have harmonism as well, sharing similar facial proportions.

The prima copulist link

Elton John's parents divorced when Elton was 14 years old. His father, who served in the Royal Air Force, wanted his son to follow him into the RAF or to work in a bank.

His mother Sheila, who was primarily responsible for his upbringing, had very different ideas: she encouraged his precocious musical talent. In the photographs below the likeness between David Furnish and Sheila is evident, with the same shape of the eye, eyebrow, and mouth. In fact, David looks more like Sheila than her own son does. Elton is lucky to have found harmonism, echoism, and prima copulism with his partner.

Prince Naruhito and Princess Masako

No matter in which race or culture it occurs, prima copulist love is not deterred by practicalities. With echoism and harmonism also present, Prince Naruhito was determined in his pursuit of Princess Masako in spite of her rebuffs.

Masako was a multilingual Harvard graduate and a second-generation diplomat who was both intelligent and assertive. She met Naruhito, heir to the throne of Japan, when she was 22, at which time she was unwilling to have a relationship with him. Naruhito, undaunted, waited six years before renewing his suit. Within two months she was won over and accepted his proposal, although she was keenly aware that as a commoner she could meet with the same reception as his mother had a generation earlier. Empress Michiko, who was also a commoner, had encountered great hostility when she married Emperor Akihito.

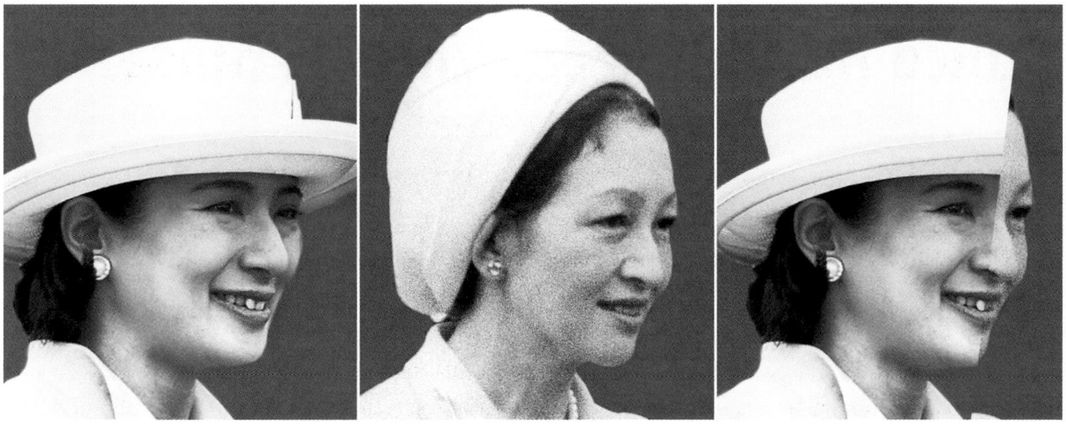

It was the first time that a member of the Japanese imperial family had married a career woman, but prima copulist love is stronger than dynastic considerations. On December 1, 2001, the couple had their first child, a daughter.

Naruhito and Masako (opposite) have echoism and harmonism. Their eyes and mouth are a similar shape, and they have the same facial proportions. The photographs on this page show that Masako is Naruhito's prima copulist love as well. Apart from the physical likenesses that can be seen between Michiko (below left, as a young woman, and above center) and Masako, the two women share a similar bearing and both radiate serenity, gentleness, and composure. The look that Naruhito responded to is not just in their faces but in their demeanor, too.

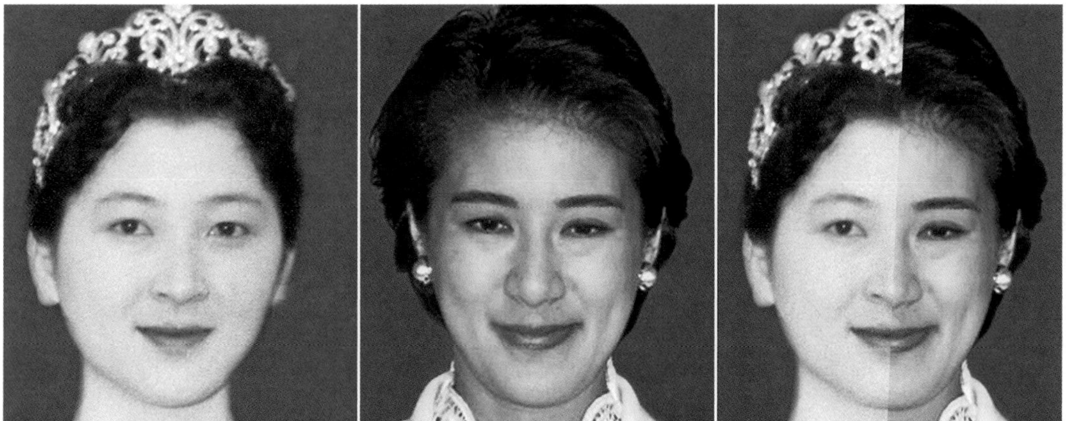

*Naruhito and Masako have **echoism** and **harmonism**, with eyes and mouth of a **similar shape** and the same **facial proportions**.*

Crown Prince Haakon and Mette-Marit

A classic example of prima copulism is seen in this engagement photograph of Crown Prince Haakon of Norway and Mette-Marit Tjessem Høiby (center). His parents understood the relationship despite the fact that Mette-Marit was a commoner and the unmarried mother of a four-year-old son, whose father had been in prison for drug offences.

The two women standing on either side of Mette-Marit are her mother, Marit Tjessem (left), and her future mother-in-law, Queen Sonja (right). There is a marked resemblance between Mette-Marit and her mother-in-law: if asked which of the two women is her mother, many people would pick out Queen Sonja rather than Marit Tjessem.

The photographs above and below show how much more closely Mette-Marit resembles her mother-in-law (below) than her mother (above). The jawline and chin of mother and daughter in particular are different and, although the shape of the mouth is a little similar, the resemblance between them is not marked. Mette-Marit and Queen Sonja share the same jawline, mouth, and chin: the lower half of their combined faces looks like a seamless whole of the same person. The length of the forehead, the distance between the nose and mouth, and the distance between the mouth and chin are all the same.

Queen Sonja was Crown Prince Haakon's first bond, and Mette-Marit resembles her. It is safe to assume, therefore, that Mette-Marit is Crown Prince Haakon's prima copulist match.

> Shortly before **their wedding**, Crown Prince Haakon told a **press conference**, **"What we two** found together was so strong that **I could not let it go**."

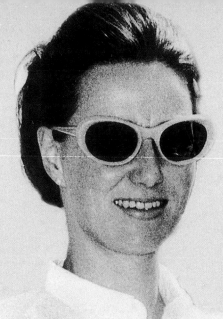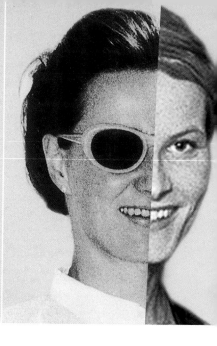

In prima copulist love, what is pertinent is how the first bond looked when she was the same age as the prima copulist match is now. These photographs show a younger Queen Sonja and Mette-Marit. The shape of the head, face, and jawline are so similar that they look almost like the same person. The likeness is most apparent in their wide smile with its unusual downward turn at the corners. When the eyes are removed from the equation (where the Queen is wearing sunglasses), the similarity of their smile comes into stronger focus. The features that Mette-Marit shares with the Queen are also those that she has in common with Crown Prince Haakon.

Mette-Marit is thus his echoist and harmonist love as well as being his prima copulist match. Their echoism is seen particularly in the jawline, cheek contours, and in the characteristic smile with the down-turned twist at the corners. Their harmonism is evident in their facial proportions: the length of the forehead and the distance from the mouth to the chin.

Three days before their wedding, Crown Prince Haakon said, "What we two found together was so strong that I could not let it go." When two people share all three visual love categories, their bond is likely to overcome all obstacles.

In conclusion

Men who resemble their mothers are more likely than others to find all three visual love groups in one person. If the man resembles both his mother and his echoist-harmonist love, it is reasonable to suppose that his echoist-harmonist love will also resemble his mother. This can work in the same way with women who resemble their fathers.

The intermingling of prima copulist, harmonist, and echoist love is a force to be reckoned with; when two people "have it all," love reigns supreme. Mette-Marit (not the most obvious choice of partner for the prince) had worked as a waitress and strawberry picker, been a "wild child," and was reported to have attended parties where drugs were used (most Norwegians find drug use unacceptable). The royal family's popularity waned, but Crown Prince Haakon found an ally in his father, King Harald, who had himself endured a wait of nine years before being granted permission to marry Sonja Haraldsen, the daughter of a shopkeeper.

It ended in **humiliation** and pain: **why risk** everything for an **illicit** affair?

Bill Clinton and **Monica Lewinsky**

President Bill Clinton had emerged from four years of public battering when he blew out the candles on his 49th birthday cake. He could ill afford more scandal about his private life—yet a few weeks later, he embarked upon an affair that was to cost him dearly.

Washington, D.C., August 9, 1995. A departure ceremony on the south lawn of the White House. President Bill Clinton is shaking hands with supporters waiting by the rope line to the presidential helicopter. One of them is a young and attractive White House intern—Monica Lewinsky. The occasion is recorded for posterity in Andrew Morton's book *Monica's Story*. "He gave me the full Bill Clinton ... when it was time to shake my hand ... the rest of the crowd disappeared and we shared an intense but brief sexual exchange." Some while after their affair began, Bill recalled that moment for Monica as they sat in the Oval Office. "I knew that one day I would kiss you," he said.

Strong love

Trauma has always been a part of Bill Clinton's life. His father, W. J. Blythe II, was killed in a car accident three months before Bill's birth. His newly widowed mother, Virginia, returned to live with her parents in Hope, Arkansas, where grandmother Edith ruled with an iron fist. Bill was just five months old when his mother went to train as a nurse anesthetist in New Orleans, leaving him in the care of his grandparents.

Virginia did not return to Arkansas until Bill was four years old. Shortly afterward, she married Roger Clinton, a car salesman. The family moved to Hot Springs, and Bill again experienced separation, this time from the grandmother he had come to love. Roger Clinton was an alcoholic and was frequently violent toward Virginia. Bill became his mother's protector and family peacemaker. The two formed an intense emotional bond. When Bill was 14 and could stand up to his stepfather, he warned him never to beat his mother again. Virginia finally divorced Roger but married him again some years later, as she said "not out of love but out of pity."

Sadness arose again when Bill was about seven. Following a cerebral hemorrhage, Edith was treated with morphine and became dependent on the drug. She was committed to the state asylum, described by federal officials as one of the worst institution of its kind in the country. The young Bill accompanied his mother on visits.

> *When Bill at last **admitted** the truth about **Monica** to Hillary, she hit him across the face. "My God, Bill, how could you **risk everything** for that?"*

This was an inauspicious enough start for any human being. The absence of a parent during a child's formative years can do great emotional damage, resulting in lack of confidence and self-esteem. It is all the more remarkable, therefore, that Bill Clinton went on to become president of the United States, the highest office in the land. During their six years in the White House, Bill and his first lady, Hillary, faced allegations on several issues including fraud, corruption, and sexual harrassment. In light of the pain caused by previous scandal and harsh public scrutiny, it seems inconceivable that Bill would choose to pursue a sexual liaison in the White House.

In his fascinating book *Bill and Hillary: the Marriage*, Christopher P. Andersen writes that when Clinton eventually was forced to admit the truth about Monica to Hillary, she hit him across the face. "You stupid, stupid, stupid bastard," she shouted. "My God, Bill, how could you risk everything for *that*?" Indeed, it was a question many asked. What special attraction did Monica have for Bill? Monica was a pretty young woman but nothing like the amazing beauties he had known. Did Bill subconsciously recognize himself in her (echoism)? Did he just like the way she looked and feel comfortable with her (harmonism)? Was her resemblance to his mother and first bond (prima copulism) a force too strong to resist?

Monica was finally free to speak about her affair with Bill in February 2002. Asked on CNN's *Larry King Live* how she had felt when Clinton made the statement, "I did not have sexual relations with that woman—Ms. Lewinsky," she replied, "There was part of me that felt glad ... because, at the time, I certainly didn't want him to lose his job. But there was, also, certainly, a part of me that was hurt." Her behavior toward Bill was typically echoist. She did not wish to hurt him.

Echoist similarities

When a man or woman meets their echoist match, the attraction is likely to be mutual because both will react to the easily recognizable similarities in their features. The outer person reflects the inner being: echoists therefore tend to share a mutual understanding. Observe in the photographs here how Bill and Monica's faces echo each other:

- eyebrows are like a bird's curved wing
- eyes are puffy
- upper eyelid is the same shape
- cheeks are similarly fleshy
- nose has a deep crease at either side
- base of the nose is rounded and the nostrils are a similarly neat shape
- lower lip is fleshy and juts slightly
- chin and jawline are strong

Harmonist similarities

When a man or woman meets their harmonist match, it is a subconscious pairing of two people with similar facial proportions. The couple do not look alike, but each likes the way the other looks and so feels comfortable with them. For people who are shy by nature or lacking in confidence, it is a real plus to find a partner with whom they feel physically confident. Monica was young, still smarting from an affair with a married man. Bill was at the zenith of his political career, but his life had known sadness right from the start. Observe their harmonist similarities:

- short nose
- short distance between nose and mouth
- long distance between mouth and chin
- same broad jawline

Visual mirroring

The mirroring of partners usually takes years of physical proximity and emotional closeness to develop. It is an unconscious compliment each partner pays the other. During their affair which lasted from November 1995 until May 1997, Bill and Monica met privately on fewer than 20 occasions. How did she "learn" his expression (as seen above) without the advantage of time? A possible explanation is that Monica watched extensive media footage on what the president was doing. Comic impersonators of the rich and famous do this with the objective of learning to copy expression. But Monica would have been unaware of what she was doing. Her mirroring of Bill was a deeply moving statement that showed the world the sincerity of her feelings for him.

The first bond

When a man meets a woman who resembles his first bond—prima copula—it is a unique match that cannot be replicated with any other woman. Virginia, shown above in a loving embrace with

Bill, was his first bond. The remarkable likeness between Virginia and Monica is seen opposite:

- round face with rounded chin and short neck
- wide-set eyes and similarly shaped lash line
- short, wide nose with heavy crease either side
- same distance from base of nose to front teeth

- wide mouth with a barely discernible break in the top of the upper lip
- same distance from mouth to chin

Perhaps it was this similarity that caused Bill to single out Monica from among many others that August day, that made her uniquely attractive to him. Bill's beloved mother had died of cancer in January the previous year. Was there something in Monica's likeness to Virginia that resonated with Bill's memory of his mother—the woman from whom he first learned love? The answer to the question (p. 157) may lie in the visual clues.

Do we

have it?

The premise of this book is that visual processes

may hold the key to finding love; but we have not

been trained to use these processes. This section

shows the methods for matching yourself and a

partner, using examples from within the book.

How can I tell if I have echoism with my partner?

Everyone knows at least one couple where the attraction of one to the other is mystifying. Very often that mystery can be solved by an understanding of the visual categories of love, but it is rarely possible to see at a glance into which category they fit—and the least likely people to be able to do it are the couple themselves. To tell which visual category of love you share with your partner you will need to work it out on paper, using photographs (see opposite). The instructions on the next few pages are straightforward, but it is essential to follow them meticulously.

How to get an accurate photographic likeness

Do's	Don'ts
Do be the natural, real you, with a normal, relaxed expression (no sucked-in cheeks or funny faces).	Don't wear too much makeup. None at all is best but otherwise aim for as natural a look as possible.
Do find an old photograph of yourself if your eyebrow shape has been radically altered by plucking or other cosmetic treatment.	Don't change your eyebrow shape with an eyebrow pencil—it distorts an important marker. Plucked eyebrows change the reading.
Do use an honest photograph, the one that most resembles you. You don't have to look like a movie star.	Don't expect an accurate reading if you have had cosmetic surgery or treatments that have altered the shape of your eyes or lips.
Do choose a current photograph unless you intend to match it with one of your partner taken the same number of years ago.	Don't use a photograph that minimizes a feature you dislike. That may be precisely what attracts another person to you and makes you special to them.

Step 1 Using the right photographs

You will need two photographs each of yourself and your partner. These must be taken at eye level so they have the same perspective, faces straight to camera or at exactly the same angle. Make sure the photographs (particularly if they are black and white) do not have heavy shadows that could be mistaken for contours.

SERIOUS

It is important that the two photographs have identical lighting, so it is best to take them in exactly the same spot. A diffuse light, which does not cast strong shadows, is essential. Passport photographs from a booth would be a good choice.

SMILING

The same principles apply: full face from the same position, same perspective, and same diffuse lighting, but with a smiling expression. Take the photographs quickly, before the smile becomes forced, and make sure the smile is not so broad that the eyes close.

Now you have the photographs, the fun can begin . . .

Step 2 *Scaling the photographs to the same proportions*

The woman's head will be smaller than the man's, so it will need to be scaled up. If you have a computer you can scan in the two images and expand the smaller head to match the larger one. Do not expand the image vertically or horizontally only—the proportions must be retained. The area which should be in the same proportion on both faces is the upper lip to the upper eyelid line. Use the unsmiling photograph to evaluate the distance. Alternatively, use a photocopier. To do this, buy some acetate paper and the appropriate pen from an art shop. Trace the larger head on the paper and place it over the photograph of the smaller one and it will indicate how far the photocopy machine has to expand the latter so that both are the same size. Place the acetate paper over your photocopy to make sure the size is correct.

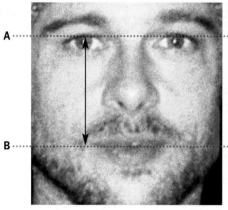
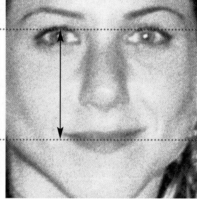

If you have done the enlargement correctly, the distance between the line where the center of the pupil hits the upper eyelid (line A) and the lipline (line B) will be the same on both faces.

Step 3 *Looking for a match: trial and error*

fold line

Fold the image of yourself in half and place it on top of your partner's. You may find that you have to fold and refold it several times. Try matching the right side of your face against the left side of your partner's face and vice versa to find out which gives the best result.

Pointers in the right direction
- Disregard the noses and lengths of chin and forehead.
- If the images do not align, readjust the size of the photographs.

Step 4 *Finding the three echoes*

When the halves of two faces are lined up, look for echoes in the shape of the brows, upper eyelid lines, and upper lip lines.

Pointers in the right direction
- Only brow and upper lip line shape are relevant, not position or thickness.
- Check both right and left sides of each face.

brow line

upper eyelid line

upper lipline

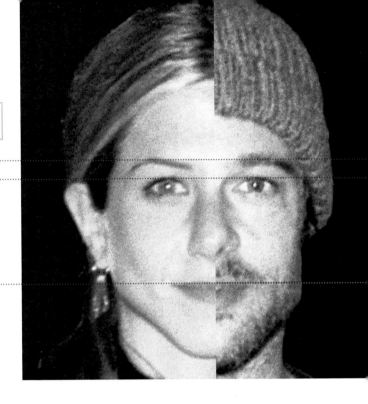

Step 5 *Doing a double check*

Sometimes the information about the mouth and upper eyelid line becomes clearer if you do the exercise with the smiling photographs: some couples look even more alike when smiling. Note that the shape of the lower lip is not relevant.

Quick check

The sunshine test
Look at old photographs taken in the sun, since shadows pick out the same contours. Notice that the face will fall into dramatic shadow around the eyelids, making the shape of the eye easier to read. In both photographs the sun should be at the same angle to the face.

How can I tell if I have **harmonism** with **my partner**?

Harmonism is harder to detect than echoism, since the couples might not look alike. Follow the method outlined for echoist matching up to Step 3, but this time fold the photograph diagonally.

Step 1 *Scaling up*

The distance from the upper eyelid to the lipline should be the same. You should not open your mouth or grimace when the photograph is taken, since this will affect the distance between mouth and chin.

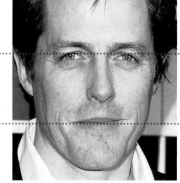
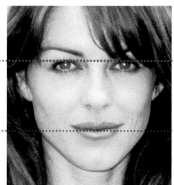

Step 2 *Looking for a match*

Fold one photograph diagonally and place it on top of the other. Try changing the angle of the fold and matching opposite sides of the faces.

The diagonal line should cross over the skull shape, skimming the side of the nose, which is largely soft tissue, rather than part of the skeleton.

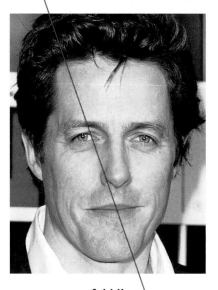

fold line

Step 3 *Measuring up*

Compare the ratios of the sections of the face shown by the red lines. The photographs must be accurately scaled; double check by comparing the upper eyelid lines and liplines.

Pointers in the right direction
- Measure from lower eyelid to base of nose, not the fleshy tip.
- Measure from base of nose to lipline.
- Measure from lipline to edge of chin
- In addition, take a diagonal measurement from lower eyelid to center of lipline.

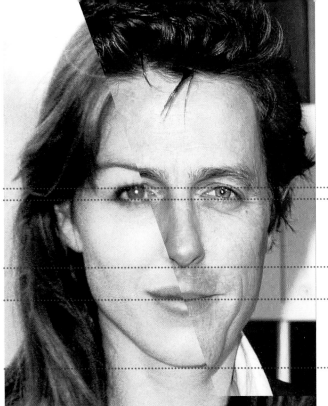

Scaling-up line

Lower eyelid line to base of nose

Nose to lipline

Lipline to edge of chin

Step 4 *Using a different angle*

While it is more difficult, lining up the faces at a three-quarter angle (semiprofile) sometimes gives a more accurate reading. When the faces are at this angle the dividing line should be directly vertical rather than diagonal.

Quick check

The cheek contour check
If one of you has a short-chinned round face and the other a long-chinned thin face you cannot have harmonism, since harmonists have the same skull shape. In order to do a quick check, turn the head until the nose goes out of view and you have a cheek contour that gives an instant outline of the chin and forehead shape. If from this angle the couple look similar there is a strong possibility that they are harmonists.

The frontal check
You can check from the front, too. If the forehead and chin appear to be the same length on both photographs, it is often an indication of harmonism.

Am I his **prima copulist** love?

When a man meets a woman who looks like his mother, the similarity is usually obvious to him, and within a short while of the meeting he may say something to that effect. But this does not necessarily mean that his mother was his first bond. If he was separated from her for much of the time while he was a baby, his grandmother, aunt, older sister, or nanny may have played a central role in his life and thus become his first bond instead. You may need to find out more about his family circumstances before you discover the identity of this significant person.

Step 1 Finding the first bond	*Step 2* Photographing yourself
To find out if you resemble his first bond, look for photographs of her taken at the time the bond was formed. The young woman he bonded with as a child may not resemble the person she is now. Wedding and baptismal photographs are excellent, and are usually taken within a few years of each other. If not, be careful when using a wedding photograph, as her appearance may have changed in the meantime.	**Once you have succeeded** in obtaining some good photographs of his first bond, take some of yourself from the same angle. Pay particular attention to whether the first bond was photographed from above or below and try to get the same camera position as accurately as you can. You may need to have the photographs of the first bond on hand so that you can cross-reference for accuracy.

Quick tips for greater accuracy

Do's	Don'ts
Ask yourself if you might look like this person when you are older. Could she have looked like you when she was younger?	Don't be afraid to ask your partner if he sees a similarity and if so where it it is. In this highly subjective category you may need help.
Ask her a few questions. Were her eyebrows plucked? Are they much changed? If so, ignore the eyebrow and use only the lid and lipline for comparison.	Don't forget that it is the "look" of the person that is most important in this category. This can often be judged without comparing photographs.

Step 3 *Scaling up to look for a prima copulist match*

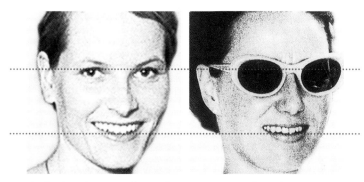

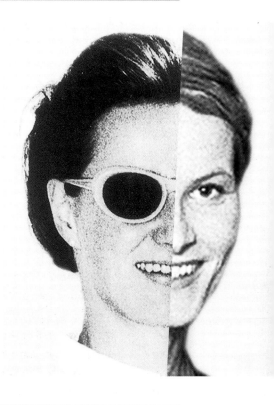

Scale the photographs to the same proportion, then compare the three echoes (sweep of eyebrow, upper eyelid, and upper lipline) that define echoism. If the prima copula figure is wearing large sunglasses you will have to go by the lipline alone. Try to use smiling photographs as well as serious ones, since the characteristic "look" of a person is often carried in the smile.

Pointers in the right direction
• Candid and informal photographs, for example vacation photos, often reveal more about a person's "look" than posed ones.

Step 4 *Using present-day photographs*

If the person with whom the man first bonded is still alive and her likeness is not much changed, you can take photographs of her and do the echoist check with those. If you cannot find a likeness by comparing the faces from the front, you can take photographs from different positions, so long as the eyes are looking at the same fixed point. Remember the similar "look" between you and your partner's first bond can be found anywhere on the face.

> **Step 5** *The triple test*

To check if you and your partner have prima copulism and echoism (or indeed all three love categories, as do the couple below) you will need to compare photographs of all three parties—you, your partner, and his first bond.

Pointers in the right direction
- Try to be photographed with the first bond and your partner standing side by side in the sunshine so that the contours of your faces are thrown into shadow.

Am I her prima copulist love?

The same do's and don'ts provided on page 172 for the female prima copulist apply here—although it will probably not be necessary to ask the male prima copulist questions about plucking his eyebrows.

A woman may be attracted to a man who resembles her first male bond. A test to find out if this is so can be carried out in exactly the same way as for the female prima copulist.

Use old photographs of the male first bond (who will probably be her father) at the time the bond was established with a photograph of yourself taken from the same angle.

If the first bond's face has not changed much over the years, photographs can be taken of both of you. This is a bonus, as it gives you the opportunity to research both of your faces from a variety of angles, looking left and right, taking a three-quarter view, tilting your heads slightly upward and slightly downward. Remember that the eyes should always be looking at the same point.

In conclusion

At the beginning of the book the three visual love groups—echoism, harmonism, and prima copulism—and the nonvisual love group, slow love, were explained. Slow love grows over time and gives a person a chance to know fully the person with whom they have come to identify. They recognize their personal qualities and begin to love them from the inside outward. With conventional dating, this opportunity does not exist. The social arena is visual and responses are necessarily quick. However, as is shown in this book, when it comes to love those visual responses are based on something deeper than basic attraction. We react as if by instinct to people whose facial proportions are the same as our own, whose features mirror ours, or whose appearance stirs a deep memory of the person who first offered us love and care.

What do our photographs reveal, and might they help us toward understanding the dynamic within our own family? Does echoism, the close friendships of like types, exist within the family circle? Given that we know the relationships of grandparents, aunts, and uncles, may we understand them further in the light of our knowledge of the information on their faces? Perhaps you may wish to use this book to analyze not only your own love relationship but also other relationships within your family.

Meeting your echoist, harmonist, or prima copulist match is exciting, but try not to lose your critical faculty. Just because you appear to have met your visual match, you must not overlook your partner's character. You should not assume that a person's facial similarity to you means they are similar in kindness or integrity, for example. In addition, be aware of the dominance or submissiveness shown in the chin (see pp. 32–33) that affects the balance of power in a relationship. Does this person allow you to lead or lean as you would like?

So often, in an endeavor to be lovable, individuals try to change in order to fulfill what they imagine the requirements of their partners to be—and this can be at the expense of their self-esteem. When one is successfully matched there is no need to adapt. One can love and be loved by another without losing oneself in the process. The joy of being able to be one's true self might be the greatest gift—and reward— of truly loving and being loved.

Acknowledgments

Author's acknowledgments

Part of the pleasure in completing this book is the opportunity to thank all those who helped me bring it to publication. I would like to thank Mary-Clare Jerram for her enthusiasm and confidence, Gillian Roberts for her marvelous gift with words, Diana Rayner for her high professionalism, Karen Sawyer for her patience and diligence, Jo Grey and Mel Watson for their painstaking work, and Catherine Bell, Serena Stent, and Antony Melville for their kindness and encouragement. My thanks also to Vladek, who helped me shape the book in its original form. I would like to thank John and Audi Bayley and Rhianon Trowell for their great help. I would like to thank all the members of my family, and Sarat and Anita, for their support and help; thanks also to Dave Thompson and Lelina Rafique. Special thanks to Richard Lowe for his help and for commenting on aspects of the original text. I am fortunate in having the wonderful Robert Kirby at PFD as my literary agent.

Agency pictures

Dorling Kindersley would like to thank the following for their kind permission to reproduce their pictures.
(t=top, b=bottom, c=center, l=left, r=right)
All Action 163 insert
Alpha Press, London 31, 88–89, 126; Dave Benett 32r, 74t; Karwai Tang 82; Nina Prommer/Globe 32l
Associated Press AP 77t, 124tr & br, 160r & tl, 161–163
Atlantic Syndication 90–91
Courtesy of John Bayley 97–98
Big Pictures 30br, tcr & tl, 80, 85b
Bridgeman Art Library, London/New York 106–109, 134c & tl
Camera Press, London Keystone 59, 169br; Mark Shenley 43r & bl; Scanpix 152–153, 154tl, tr, bc & bcr, 173tl, tr, bl & br; Stewart Mark 148; Tom Hanley 73; Theodore Wood 26r, 27 r, 170tr, bc, 171 tl
Corbis 112c & bl; Bob Linder/Corbis Sygma 79c & cl, 167br, 169bl
Hulton Archive/Getty Images 2tl, cr & bl, 52–55, 62r & bl, 63c & tr, 65, 68c & bl, 69–72, 84t, 85t, 116, 117c & br, 118l, 119 tl & br, 124tl & bl, 134r & bl, 135, 137, 140, 151tc & bl , 154tc, bl & bcr, 173tc
In-Focus Photographic Agency Richard Maw 22t, 23r
Katz/FSP 114l

Kobal Collection 129r
Korpa Press/Pep Bosch 112t & br
London Features International CPS/LFI 2tr & bc, 76, 77b, 142r; David Fisher/LFI 40r, 41r, 122r, 142l, 160c & bl; David Koppel/LFI 92tl & tcr; Gregg de Guire 28cl & r, 83, 84b, 171br; Kevin Mazur-Umaz/LFI 92bl & br; Marc Larkin/LFI 93cl & r; Nicolas Khayat/ABACA/LFI 40l, 41l; Desmond O'Neill: 118r, 119tr & bl, 120, 121l
Press Association Photos 2cl & br, 18l, 20c & bl, 21l, 22b, 23l, 24l, 30tcl, tr & bl, 42, 43c & tl, 46–50, 58, 62tr & c, 63r & bl, 74b, 92tc & tr, 93bl & bcr, 113, 114r, 121r, 122l, 151tl, tr, bc & br
Popperfoto.com 141
Retna Pictures Ltd Steve Granitz 2c, 146l, 147r
Reuters 79bl& br, 167bl, 169bc
Rex Features Araldo di Crollalanza 28l & cr, 171 bl; Consolidated News 159r & bl; David Hartley 24r; Erik Pendzich 26tl & bl, 27l, 159c & tl, 170tl, bl, bcl & br, 171tr; Jason Shillingford 78, 79t; 167t, 168, 169t; Malcolm Gilson 64l; Matt Baron 81; Mike Webster 149c & bl; Richard Young 146r, 147l, 149r & tl; Rooke/Kyriacou 155, 174;
Sipa Press 66, 125, 150; Snap 68t & br, 132;
Stills Press Agency 130r, 131r; Tim Rooke 2tc, 18r, 20r & tl, 21br, 117 t & bl; Tony Larkin 64r
Courtesy of Rhianon Trowell & Marian Mastroianni 128, 129l, 130l, 131l
UKPress 75

Quotations

p. 11 *Falling in Love* Ayala Malach Pines (Routledge, New York, 2000)
The Conquest of Happiness Bertrand Russell (Routledge, London, 1975)
p. 62 *The Path to Power* Margaret Thatcher (HarperCollins, New York, 1995)
p. 65 *Mikhail Gorbachev: Memoirs* Mikhail Gorbachev (Doubleday, New York, 1996)
p. 96 *Iris* John Bayley (Abacus, London, 2002)
p. 117 *The Prince of Wales: A Biography* Jonathan Dimbleby (William Morrow, New York, 1994)
p. 125 *The Kennedy Curse: Why America's First Family Has Been Haunted by Tragedy for 150 Years* Edward Klein (Saint Martin's Press, New York, 2003)
p. 127 *Richard Burton: A Brother Remembered* David Jenkins (Trafalgar Square, North Pomfret, 1994)
p. 128 *A Christmas Story* Richard Burton (W. W. Norton, New York, 1991)
p. 157 *Monica's Story* Andrew Morton (Saint Martin's Press, New York, 1999)
p. 158 *Bill and Hillary: The Marriage* Christopher P. Andersen (William Morrow, New York, 1999)